Alhambra Travel

GUIDE

2024 EDITION

Discover and unlock the secrets of
Alhambra Rich
Heritage, Architectural Marvel and
vibrant Culture

Jack X. Woodburn

Copyright © 2024 Jack X. Woodburn

All Rights Reserved

All rights reserved. No part of this book may be reproduced, stored, or transmitted in any form or by any means, electronic, mechanical, photocopying, recording, scanning, or otherwise, without prior written permission from the publisher.

**In loving memory of my wonderful Wife
who loved this beautiful place.**

Table of content

IMPORTANT NOTE
BEFORE READING
Chapter One
Introduction
    The Historical Significance of Alhambra
    Alhambra's Influence on Spanish and Islamic Architecture
    The Symbolism and Mysticism of Alhambra
Chapter Two
Planning Your Alhambra Adventure
    Understanding Granada: Getting to Know the City of Alhambra
    Exploring Granada's Cultural and Historical Background
    Climate and Best Times to Visit Granada
    Practical Information for Travelers
Chapter Three
Navigating Alhambra: Tips and Essential Information
    Alhambra's Layout and Key Areas to Explore
    Ticketing, Entry Times, and Visitor Regulations
    Guided Tours and Audio Guides
Chapter Four
Exploring Alhambra's Architectural Wonders
    The Alhambra Complex: An Architectural Overview

    The Alcazaba: Fortress and First Line of Defense
    The Nasrid Palaces: Royal Residences of Alhambra
    The Generalife: Gardens and Summer Retreat

Chapter Five

The Nasrid Palaces: Jewel of Alhambra
    The Court of the Myrtles: Beauty and Serenity
    The Palace of the Lions: A Masterpiece of Islamic Art
    The Palace of Charles V: The Blend of Christian and Islamic Styles

Chapter Six

Discovering Alhambra's Cultural Heritage
    Alhambra's Cultural Significance: A Tapestry of Influences
    Islamic Art and Architecture in Alhambra
    Moorish Influence on Spanish Culture
    UNESCO World Heritage Status and Preservation Efforts

Chapter Seven

The Alhambra Museum: Treasures from the Past
    The Museum's Collections and Exhibits
    Notable Artefacts and Historical Objects
    Exploring the Museum's Interactive Displays

Chapter Eight

Beyond Alhambra: Exploring Granada
    The Albayzin: Granada's Historic Neighbourhood
    Exploring the Albayzin's Narrow Streets and Stunning Views

- The Sacromonte: Flamenco and Gypsy Culture
- Tapas Bars and Culinary Delights in Granada

Chapter Nine

Day Trips from Granada: Unveiling Nearby Gems
- The Sierra Nevada: Spain's Pristine Mountain Range
- The Alpujarras: Picturesque Villages and Natural Beauty
- The Caves of Guadix: Underground Wonders

Chapter Ten

Conclusion
- Making the Most of Your Alhambra Experience
- Insider Tips for an Enriching Visit
- Preserving Alhambra's Legacy for Future Generations

IMPORTANT NOTE BEFORE READING

You might find a special trip experience in these pages.

The purpose of this alhambra guide is to inspire your creativity, imagina-tion, and sense of adventure.

Since we think that the beauty of every discovery should be experienced firsthand, free from visual filter and prejudices, you won't find any pictures here.

Every monument, every location, and every secret nook are waiting for you when you get there, eager to surprise and amaze you.

Why should we ruin the wonder and excitement of the initial impression? Prepare to set off on a voyage where your imagination will serve as both your single mode of transportation and your personal tour guide. Keep in mind that your own creations are the most attractive.

This book lacks a map and photographs, in contrast to many other manuals.

Why? Because in our opinion the best discoveries are made when a person gets lost, let themselves go with the flow of the environment, and embraces the ambiguity of the road.

Be cautious, trust your gut, and expect the unexpected. In a world without maps, where roads are made with each step you take, the magic of the voyage starts now.

Chapter One

Introduction

The Historical Significance of Alhambra

The Alhambra, a UNESCO World Heritage Site nestled in the heart of Granada, Spain, is not just a palace and fortress complex; it is a living testament to the ebb and flow of history, reflecting the confluence of Islamic, Christian, and Renaissance influences. Its historical significance unfolds as a captivating tale of cultural exchange, artistic brilliance, and political transformations.

Constructed in the mid-13th century by the Nasrid Dynasty, the Alhambra emerged during the final chapter of Islamic rule in the Iberian Peninsula. Facing the encroaching forces of the Reconquista, the Nasrid rulers sought to create a refuge that transcended mere fortification.

The very name "Alhambra," derived from the Arabic "Al-Hamra," meaning "The Red One," alludes to the reddish hue of its walls, setting the stage for the captivating aesthetics within.

At its core, the Alhambra is an architectural masterpiece that seamlessly blends functionality with intricate artistry. The Nasrid Palaces, characterized by geometric patterns, intricate tilework, and delicate stucco decorations, showcase the zenith of Islamic architecture.

The Court of the Lions, with its iconic fountain surrounded by twelve marble lions, stands as a testament to the Nasrids' ingenuity in water engineering and their commitment to creating paradisiacal spaces.

In 1492, the Catholic Monarchs, Ferdinand and Isabella, completed the Reconquista by capturing Granada. Rather than eradicating the Alhambra, they recognized its architectural prowess and adapted it for Christian use.

This adaptive approach is evident in the addition of a Renaissance palace by Charles V within the complex, symbolizing the evolution of the site through changing political and cultural landscapes.

The Alhambra's historical significance extends beyond its architectural splendor to the intellectual and cultural legacy it embodies. The intricate inscriptions adorning its walls include verses from the Quran, poetic expressions, and philosophical musings, offering a glimpse into the intellectual richness of the Nasrid era.

Scholars from various backgrounds converged within the Alhambra, fostering an environment where different cultural traditions coexisted and thrived.

The subsequent centuries witnessed shifts in ownership and purpose for the Alhambra. Neglected in the 18th century and facing natural disasters, it fell into disrepair.

However, the 19th-century Romantic movement sparked a renewed interest in the Alhambra, as poets, writers, and artists celebrated its exotic allure. This cultural renaissance contributed to a growing awareness of the need for preservation.

The 20th century marked a pivotal era for the Alhambra as extensive restoration efforts sought to revive its former glory. UNESCO's recognition in 1984 as a World Heritage Site validated its universal cultural value and emphasized the collective responsibility to safeguard this historical gem.

Today, visitors to the Alhambra embark on a journey through time, traversing the intricate chambers of the Nasrid Palaces, exploring the lush Generalife gardens, and marveling at the panoramic views of Granada from the Alcazaba fortress.

The Alhambra's significance lies not only in its architectural grandeur but in its ability to transport visitors to a bygone era where different cultures converged and flourished.

The Generalife gardens, with their meticulously planned layout, fountains, and greenery, provide a tranquil retreat, emphasizing the Nasrids' appreciation for the harmony between the artificial and the natural.

Each step within the Alhambra's walls resonates with echoes of rulers, scholars, and artists who left an indelible mark on the cultural landscape of medieval Spain.

The historical significance of the Alhambra transcends its physical beauty; it encapsulates the dynamic interplay of civilizations, the resilience of cultural heritage, and the enduring legacy of human creativity.

As a cultural mosaic, the Alhambra invites visitors to immerse themselves in a narrative that spans centuries, acknowledging the intertwined threads of history that have shaped this iconic site into a timeless symbol of cultural diversity and artistic excellence.

Alhambra's Influence on Spanish and Islamic Architecture

The Alhambra, an architectural marvel situated beautifully at Granada, Spain, serves as an exquisite fusion of Spanish and Islamic design, leaving an indelible mark on the course of both architectural traditions.

This fortress and palace complex, built during the Nasrid Dynasty in the 13th century, stands not only as a symbol of the Nasrids' sophistication but also as a source of inspiration that transcends cultural and temporal boundaries.

The Alhambra's influence on Spanish architecture is profound, shaping the aesthetic sensibilities of the region for centuries. The palace's iconic horseshoe arches, characterized by their distinctive pointed shape resembling a horseshoe, became a hallmark of Islamic architecture and left an enduring impact on Spanish design.

These arches, found throughout the Alhambra, impart a sense of elegance and rhythm to its spaces, setting a precedent for their integration into subsequent Spanish structures.

Moreover, the Alhambra introduced the concept of the "Patio" to Spanish architecture. The central courtyards adorned with meticulously designed gardens became a defining feature of the palace. This notion of creating harmonious, enclosed spaces with a focus on aesthetics and tranquility found its way into the architecture of later Spanish palaces and homes.

The influence of the Alhambra's courtyards can be observed in the serene inner spaces of structures like the Generalife gardens, where water features and greenery create an oasis-like ambiance.

The intricate art of muqarnas, characterized by its honeycomb-like vaulting, is another contribution of the Alhambra to Spanish architecture. These elaborate geometric designs adorn ceilings and domes, adding a sense of depth and complexity to the visual experience.

The interplay of light and shadow on muqarnas surfaces became a distinctive feature, influencing the aesthetics of subsequent Spanish structures and contributing to the ornate detailing seen in cathedrals and palaces.

As the Reconquista unfolded and Islamic and Christian cultures coexisted, the Alhambra played a pivotal role in shaping the Mudejar architectural style. Mudejar, marked by the use of Islamic decorative elements in Christian buildings, reflects the cultural exchange that occurred during this period.

The Giralda in Seville, originally a minaret converted into a bell tower, showcases the fusion inspired by the Alhambra, with its incorporation of Islamic patterns and arches reminiscent of the palace.

The Alhambra's influence transcends its immediate historical context, reaching into the Spanish Renaissance and Gothic periods. Elements such as intricate ornamentation, geometric patterns, and the use of arabesques became integral to these architectural styles.

The legacy of the Alhambra lives on in the detailing of cathedrals like the Cathedral of Granada, where echoes of Islamic influence can be traced in the delicately carved stonework and geometric motifs.

On the other side of the spectrum, the Alhambra's impact on Islamic architecture is equally profound. Its legacy resonates in the continued use of geometric patterns, arabesques, and calligraphy in Islamic structures globally.

The palace's intricate tilework, known as azulejos, has become a recurring feature in Islamic art, adorning mosques, palaces, and homes across diverse regions. The Alhambra, in essence, serves as a source of inspiration for architects and artisans in the Islamic world, exemplifying the harmony between aesthetics and functionality.

The Symbolism and Mysticism of Alhambra

The Alhambra, perched majestically atop a hill in Granada, Spain, is not merely a collection of palaces and fortifications; it is a living testament to the profound symbolism and mysticism woven into its every stone.

As you enter this architectural marvel, you embark on a journey through the corridors of time, where each element whispers a story of cultural fusion, religious devotion, and a mystical connection to the divine.

At the heart of the Alhambra's symbolism is the delicate dance of light and shadow, a spectacle orchestrated by its intricate lattice work, or "jaali." This geometric web filters sunlight into mesmerizing patterns, creating a play of chiaroscuro that evokes the Islamic concept of divine light.

This interplay symbolizes the transcendent journey, where shadows represent the material world, and light signifies the spiritual realm. As visitors wander through the palaces, they become participants in this celestial ballet, enveloped in an atmosphere that transcends the mundane.

The Nasrid Palaces, adorned with stucco ornamentation, epitomize aniconism – the avoidance of representational art in Islamic tradition. Instead, the walls breathe life through intricate geometric patterns and calligraphy.

This deliberate absence of human or animal figures directs attention to the divine, fostering a contemplative environment. The arabesques tell tales not just of aesthetics but of a profound connection to spirituality, where the act of creation becomes an act of devotion.

The Court of the Lions stands as a symbolic masterpiece within the Alhambra. The twelve lions supporting a central fountain symbolize strength and power, while the twelve channels of water represent the twelve tribes of Israel.

This fusion of Islamic and Jewish symbolism reflects the harmonious coexistence of different cultures during Andalusia's medieval period. The court becomes a stage where diverse traditions converge, transcending religious boundaries and emphasizing shared humanity.

The Hall of the Abencerrajes, with its captivating dome and star-shaped skylights, adds an element of mysticism to the Alhambra's narrative. Legend intertwines with architecture as tales circulate about a tragic event within these walls – the murder of members of the Abencerrajes family.

The star-shaped openings are said to represent the bloodied destiny of these individuals. The mystique surrounding this hall invites contemplation on the echoes of history, turning architecture into a vessel for storytelling.

Venturing into the Alhambra's gardens, particularly the Generalife, one steps into an earthly paradise. The meticulous arrangement of flora, fountains, and pathways mirrors the Islamic vision of paradise on earth.

The sound of water flowing, coupled with the scent of blossoms, creates an immersive experience that transcends the physical realm, evoking a sense of harmony and divine beauty. The gardens become a manifestation of the eternal pursuit of the idyllic, a glimpse into the spiritual yearning for a perfect existence.

Azulejos, the intricate tilework that graces the Alhambra's walls, is a canvas of symbolism. Geometric patterns represent the divine order and the infinite, while Arabic calligraphy often bears verses from the Quran, infusing the space with sacred text.

The choice of colors in the tiles is deliberate, with blues and greens symbolizing the divine, reds embodying earthly passions, and white representing purity. Every tile becomes a brushstroke in a masterpiece that transcends visual aesthetics, inviting visitors to delve into layers of meaning.

Beyond its Islamic symbolism, the Alhambra embodies a broader narrative of religious and cultural coexistence. The Christian monarchs who conquered the Alhambra recognized its significance and preserved its Islamic features, exemplifying a respect for cultural heritage.

The fusion of Islamic, Christian, and Jewish influences within the Alhambra's walls mirrors the broader historical context of Andalusia, where diverse communities coexisted and contributed to a golden age of intellectual and artistic flourishing.

Chapter Two

Planning Your Alhambra Adventure

Understanding Granada: Getting to Know the City of Alhambra

As you plan your Alhambra adventure, taking the time to understand Granada will deepen your appreciation for the city that cradles this iconic palace and fortress complex.

Historical Tapestry:

Granada's history is a tapestry woven with threads of Islamic rule, Christian conquest, and cultural synthesis. The city's prominence soared during the Nasrid Dynasty, culminating in the construction of the Alhambra in the 13th century.

The Reconquista, led by Catholic Monarchs Ferdinand and Isabella, witnessed the fall of Granada in 1492, marking a pivotal moment in Spanish history. The echoes of this complex past resonate through Granada's streets, blending

Moorish and Spanish influences into a unique cultural amalgamation.

Navigating the Albayzín:

The Albayzín, Granada's historic Muslim quarter, is a labyrinth of narrow alleys, whitewashed houses, and hidden squares. As you wander through this UNESCO World Heritage site, you'll discover a microcosm of Andalusian history.

The intricate Moorish architecture, reminiscent of the Alhambra, creates an immersive atmosphere, transporting you to a bygone era. Lose yourself in the Albayzín's maze, where each turn unveils a new facet of Granada's captivating past.

Tapas Culture:

Granada boasts a unique culinary tradition deeply rooted in its vibrant social life. The city is renowned for its tapas culture, where complimentary small dishes accompany your drinks.

Exploring the local taverns and bars allows you to savor a variety of Andalusian flavors, from savory olives to delectable chorizo. The lively atmosphere of these establishments mirrors the convivial spirit that defines Granada's social scene.

Sacromonte's Flamenco Heritage:

Venture into Sacromonte, perched on the hills overlooking Granada, and you'll be immersed in the soul-stirring world of Flamenco. This historic neighborhood, famous for its cave dwellings, is synonymous with the passionate rhythms and expressive dance of Flamenco.

Attend a Flamenco show in one of Sacromonte's intimate venues to experience the raw emotion and artistic prowess that define this traditional Andalusian art form.

The Majestic Alhambra:

Of course, no exploration of Granada is complete without delving into the crown jewel of the city – the Alhambra. Perched atop the Sabika Hill, this palatial complex is a testament to the grandeur of Islamic architecture and the Nasrid Dynasty's sophisticated taste.

Marvel at the intricate stucco work, stroll through the Generalife Gardens, and stand in awe of the panoramic views of Granada from the Alcazaba fortress. To ensure your visit is seamless, secure your tickets in advance, allowing you to savor the Alhambra's beauty at your own pace.

Romantic Views from Mirador de San Nicolás:

For a postcard-perfect view of the Alhambra, head to the Mirador de San Nicolás. This scenic viewpoint in the Albayzín offers a breathtaking panorama, with the Alhambra framed against the backdrop of the Sierra Nevada mountains. Sunset paints the sky in hues of orange and pink, casting a warm glow over the Alhambra and creating a scene that feels straight out of a dream.

Sierra Nevada Adventure:

Granada's proximity to the Sierra Nevada mountains opens the door to outdoor adventures. If time allows, consider a day trip to Sierra Nevada National Park for hiking or skiing, depending on the season.

The snow-capped peaks and pristine landscapes provide a striking contrast to the historical richness of Granada, offering a well-rounded experience for nature enthusiasts.

Transportation Hub:

Granada's strategic location makes it easily accessible for travelers. The Federico García Lorca Granada-Jaén Airport connects the city to major European destinations.Granada's efficient public transportation system, including buses and taxis, ensures convenient travel within the city and its surroundings.

Cultural Festivals:

Timing your visit to coincide with Granada's vibrant festivals enhances the cultural experience. The Corpus Christi celebrations in June and the International Festival of Music and Dance in July showcase Granada's artistic prowess.

Immerse yourself in the lively processions, flamenco performances, and concerts to witness the city's dynamic cultural spirit.

Exploring Granada's Cultural and Historical Background

Embarking on a journey to explore Granada's cultural and historical background is a captivating adventure that immerses travelers in the rich tapestry of Spain's past.

Begin your exploration with the crown jewel of Granada – the Alhambra. Rising gracefully against the backdrop of the Sierra Nevada, this UNESCO World Heritage Site is a testament to the city's Islamic heritage.

Secure your tickets in advance, allowing ample time to explore the Nasrid Palaces, the Generalife gardens, and the Alcazaba fortress. As you wander through the intricately carved halls and lush courtyards of the Alhambra, absorb the stories of the Nasrid Dynasty and marvel at the fusion of Islamic and Christian architectural elements.

Adjacent to the Alhambra lies the Albaicín, one of Granada's most historic neighborhoods. A labyrinth of narrow cobblestone streets, whitewashed houses, and hidden squares, the Albaicín transports visitors to medieval Moorish Spain.

Begin your stroll at the Plaza Nueva, and meander uphill, allowing the sensory delights of the neighborhood to unfold. Discover the Mirador de San Nicolás for a breathtaking panoramic view of the Alhambra, a moment that encapsulates the essence of Granada's architectural charm.

Continue your journey through time by exploring the Realejo, Granada's former Jewish quarter. Delve into the history of the Jewish community as you wander through its streets, uncovering remnants of synagogues and the traces of a bygone era.

Visit the Casa de los Tiros, a museum housed in a Renaissance palace, offering insights into Granada's cultural and historical evolution.

To truly grasp Granada's cultural diversity, attend a flamenco performance in the Sacromonte caves. Flamenco, a passionate and expressive art form, weaves together Gypsy, Arab, and Jewish influences.

The Sacromonte caves, with their rustic charm, provide an intimate setting for this enchanting spectacle. Allow the music and dance to transport you to the heart of Andalusian folklore, where the city's multicultural past comes alive.

No exploration of Granada's cultural tapestry is complete without a visit to the city's religious monuments. The Granada Cathedral, an imposing masterpiece of Spanish Renaissance architecture, stands as a symbol of Christian rule.

Marvel at its intricate facades and venture inside to witness the grandeur of the Royal Chapel, the final resting place of Catholic Monarchs Ferdinand and Isabella. The juxtaposition of Islamic and Christian influences becomes palpable, echoing the city's complex history.

As you traverse Granada's historic districts, savor the culinary delights that reflect the city's multicultural influences. Head to the Alcaicería, the reconstructed Moorish silk market, transformed into a bustling bazaar.

Engage your senses in the lively atmosphere, where the scent of Moroccan tea mingles with the enticing aromas of local tapas. Indulge in the culinary diversity of Granada, from traditional Andalusian dishes to Moorish-inspired flavors that showcase the city's gastronomic richness.

To gain a deeper understanding of Granada's intellectual legacy, visit the University of Granada. Founded in 1531, it is one of the oldest universities in Spain and has played a significant role in the city's cultural development.

Stroll through its historic corridors and courtyards, soaking in the ambiance of intellectual pursuits that have thrived within its walls for centuries.

As the day transitions into evening, immerse yourself in the vibrant cultural scene that defines Granada. Attend a performance at the Isabel la Católica Theater or explore the city's numerous art galleries and cultural spaces.

Granada's commitment to preserving and promoting its cultural heritage is evident in its contemporary artistic endeavors, creating a seamless connection between the past and the present.

Climate and Best Times to Visit Granada

The Seasons Unveiled

Spring: A Blossoming Canvas (March to May)

As winter gracefully yields to the embrace of spring, Granada awakens in a burst of colors and fragrances. March, April, and May bring mild temperatures, making spring an ideal time to explore the city. The Albayzín, with its narrow streets flanked by blooming bougainvillea and jasmine, becomes a living canvas of vibrant hues.

The Generalife Gardens within the Alhambra are adorned with the delicate petals of cherry blossoms and a myriad of flowers, creating a surreal backdrop to the historical splendor.

Spring is also the season when Granada hosts the International Festival of Music and Dance. The Alhambra becomes a stage for captivating performances, and the city resonates with the melodies of classical music and the rhythmic beats of Flamenco. The ambiance is one of celebration, cultural immersion, and the promise of warmer days ahead.

Summer: Sunlit Allure (June to August)

As the sun ascends to its zenith, summer blankets Granada in warmth. June marks the beginning of the high tourist season, as visitors flock to revel in the city's historical and cultural treasures. The days are long, and the evenings offer a delightful coolness, creating an enchanting atmosphere for exploration.

While the temperatures can soar, the allure of Granada's landmarks remains undiminished.

Early mornings are an ideal time to wander through the Alhambra, as the sun casts a golden glow over the Nasrid Palaces and the Generalife Gardens.

In the evenings, the Albayzín comes alive with a vibrant energy, as locals and visitors alike gather in the lively tapas bars and open-air cafes. However, for those seeking a more tranquil experience, venturing into the Albaicín's narrow streets during the siesta hours provides a peaceful escape.

Autumn: A Tapestry of Colors (September to November)

As summer gradually wanes, autumn graces Granada with a tapestry of warm colors. September and October offer a pleasant climate, with milder temperatures beckoning explorers to stroll through the city's historic quarters.

The changing leaves add a touch of magic to the Albayzín, creating a picturesque backdrop for those seeking to immerse themselves in Granada's cultural and architectural wonders.

Autumn is also an excellent time for outdoor activities, such as hiking in the nearby Sierra Nevada mountains. The crisp air and clear skies enhance the panoramic views, providing a refreshing counterpoint to the city's historical richness. With fewer crowds, this season allows for a more intimate connection with Granada's landscapes and landmarks.

Winter: A Tranquil Elegance (December to February)

Winter arrives with a sense of tranquility, casting a serene elegance over Granada. While the temperatures can be cooler, especially in the evenings, the city maintains a unique charm. December brings festive decorations, and the Albayzín glows with the warm light of holiday festivities.

Winter is an opportune time to explore indoor attractions, such as the Capilla Real, where the tombs of Ferdinand and Isabella rest in perpetual splendor. The Granada Cathedral, with its Gothic and Renaissance architecture, offers a refuge of artistic and historical richness.

The Alhambra, adorned with a subtle dusting of frost, exudes a quiet magnificence, and visitors can revel in the tranquility that comes with the off-peak season.

Choosing the Perfect Time

Shoulder Seasons: May and September

For a harmonious blend of favorable weather and fewer crowds, the shoulder seasons of May and September emerge as optimal times to visit Granada. During these months, spring or autumn delights the senses, and the city exudes a pleasant ambiance.

Exploring the Alhambra, wandering through the Albayzín, and savoring tapas in open-air cafes become immersive experiences without the peak-season hustle.

Special Events: June and July

June and July witness the International Festival of Music and Dance in Granada, transforming the city into a cultural haven.

If you're drawn to the symphony of classical music, Flamenco rhythms, and open-air performances, these months offer a unique opportunity to revel in Granada's artistic spirit. Plan your visit around these events for an enriched cultural experience.

Winter Tranquility: December to February

If you cherish a quieter exploration and a touch of winter magic, the months of December to February bring a tranquil elegance to Granada.

While the temperatures may be cooler, the city takes on a serene charm, providing an intimate setting for experiencing its historical and cultural treasures without the bustling crowds.

Respect Siesta Hours:

Embrace the local rhythm by respecting the siesta hours, typically from 2:00 PM to 5:00 PM. Many shops and businesses close during this time, making it an ideal period for a leisurely lunch or a restful break.

Local Festivals:

Check the local festival calendar to align your visit with cultural events or festivities. Participating in festivals provides a unique insight into Granada's vibrant traditions and community spirit.

Practical Information for Travelers

Booking Tickets in Advance:

The Alhambra's allure has led to high demand for entry tickets, and it's advisable to secure your tickets well in advance. The Nasrid Palaces, in particular, have limited daily entries, making pre-booking essential.

The official website or authorized ticket vendors facilitate this process, allowing you to choose specific time slots for your visit. By planning ahead, you not only ensure access to the Nasrid Palaces but also streamline your exploration of the Generalife Gardens, Alcazaba fortress, and other areas within the complex.

Arriving at the Alhambra:

Granada is well-connected, and reaching the Alhambra is convenient for travelers. The Federico García Lorca Granada-Jaén Airport serves as the primary gateway, with various international and domestic flights. From the airport, taxis, buses, and car rentals are available for the approximately 20-minute journey to the city center.

Granada's public transportation system is efficient, and buses or taxis can take you from the city center to the Alhambra complex. Alternatively, walking from the city center to the Alhambra offers a scenic route, allowing you to savor the historic charm of Granada's streets as you ascend towards the palace complex.

Accommodations in Granada:

Granada offers a range of accommodations to suit diverse preferences and budgets. From luxury hotels with panoramic views of the Alhambra to charming boutique guesthouses tucked away in the Albayzín, the city caters to every traveler's needs.

When booking your stay, consider proximity to the Alhambra, the city center, or specific neighborhoods based on your preferences for exploration and ambiance.

Navigating the Alhambra Complex:

The Alhambra's vast complex comprises multiple attractions, each deserving of attention. Crafting a well-planned itinerary ensures that you make the most of your visit.

Begin with the Nasrid Palaces, the crown jewel, and allocate sufficient time to explore their intricate details. Proceed to the Generalife Gardens, the Alcazaba fortress, and other areas, allowing each section to unfold as a distinct chapter in your Alhambra narrative.

To enhance your experience, consider hiring an official guide or using audio guides available at the entrance. These guides provide invaluable insights into the historical and architectural significance of each site, offering a deeper appreciation for the Alhambra's cultural richness.

Respecting Time Slots: Punctuality is the Key to Serenity

The Alhambra operates on a strict schedule, with designated time slots for entry to the Nasrid Palaces. Adhering to your allocated time ensures a serene and crowd-controlled exploration, enhancing your connection with the palatial surroundings.

Plan your arrival at the entrance accordingly, allowing ample time to clear security checks and immerse yourself in the enchantment of the Nasrid Palaces.

Comfortable Attire and Footwear:

Granada's climate can vary, so dressing in layers allows you to adapt to changing conditions. Comfortable footwear is essential, especially if you plan to explore the entire complex.

The Alhambra's intricate pathways, some adorned with cobblestones, are best navigated in sturdy and comfortable shoes, ensuring that every step becomes a part of your delightful journey through history.

Water and Snacks: Staying Energized for Discovery

Exploring the Alhambra requires energy, and staying hydrated is crucial, especially during warmer seasons. Carry a reusable water bottle to ensure you remain refreshed throughout your visit.

Also, packing some snacks provides a quick energy boost, allowing you to savor the experience without interruptions.

Photography Etiquette:

The Alhambra's beauty beckons for photographs, and capturing the splendor is a natural inclination. However, it's essential to be mindful of the surroundings and fellow visitors. Some areas, particularly within the Nasrid Palaces, may have restrictions on flash photography.

Embrace the opportunity to create visual memories while respecting the serene ambiance of the palatial surroundings.

Sun Protection and Sunscreen:

Granada's sun can be intense, especially during the warmer months. To shield yourself from the sun's rays, wear a hat, sunglasses, and apply sunscreen.

These simple measures ensure that your exploration of the Alhambra remains comfortable and enjoyable, allowing you to focus on the architectural marvels rather than the sun's glare.

Baggage and Large Items:

Streamline your journey by minimizing the burden you carry. Large backpacks or bags may not be allowed into certain areas, and you'll find the dance of exploration far more comfortable without cumbersome items.

Opt for smaller bags, ensuring a nimble and graceful traversal through the Alhambra's intricate passages.

Footwear:

The Alhambra's mosaic of courtyards, gardens, and halls invites you to traverse its varied terrain. Choose footwear that not only complements your attire but also provides comfort for extended periods of walking.

Your footwear should be a seamless extension of your dance, allowing you to glide through the historical stage with ease.

Rain or Shine:

Weather in Granada can be unpredictable, and your dance through the Alhambra should persist regardless of rain or shine.

Consider bringing a lightweight, packable rain jacket or umbrella if you're exploring during seasons with sporadic showers. Embracing the elements as part of your performance adds an adventurous layer to your journey.

Shopping for Souvenirs:

Before leaving the Alhambra, explore the on-site shops for unique souvenirs that capture the essence of your journey. From intricate ceramics to exquisite replicas of Moorish designs, these souvenirs serve as tangible reminders of the cultural treasures you've uncovered.

Try consider exploring local markets in Granada for authentic Andalusian crafts and mementos.

Chapter Three

Navigating Alhambra: Tips and Essential Information

Alhambra's Layout and Key Areas to Explore

As you approach the Alhambra, its silhouette against the Sierra Nevada mountains transports you to a realm where Moorish architecture weaves an enchanting tapestry of history and beauty.

Navigating the Alhambra is akin to traversing a labyrinth of palatial wonders, gardens, and fortifications.

The Nasrid Palaces: A Palatial Odyssey

The Nasrid Palaces stand as the epitome of Moorish architectural splendor, housing the intricate legacy of the Nasrid Dynasty. Begin your journey in the Mexuar, the oldest part of the palaces, where the Court of the Myrtles entices with its reflective pool and the delicate beauty of surrounding chambers.

As you progress, the Comares Palace unfolds, showcasing the resplendent Patio de los Leones (Court of the Lions) – an exquisite symphony of columns, arches, and the iconic lion fountain.

Continue your exploration into the Palacio de los Leones, where the intricate stucco work, filigree arches, and geometric patterns transport you to a realm where every detail is a testament to the Nasrids' devotion to art and beauty.

The Hall of the Abencerrajes, with its domed ceiling resembling a celestial canopy, and the Hall of the Ambassadors, where the Nasrid rulers held court, are among the highlights that await within this palatial labyrinth.

Generalife Gardens: Nature's Tranquil Embrace

Adjacent to the Nasrid Palaces, the Generalife Gardens provide a serene counterpoint to the grandeur of the palaces. These lush, terraced gardens served as a retreat for the Nasrid rulers, offering respite amidst the architectural splendor.

The Patio de la Acequia, adorned with a central water channel and meticulously landscaped greenery, creates a paradise of tranquility. Stroll through the intimate courtyards, breathe in the fragrance of blooming flowers, and savor the panoramic views of Granada from the terraces.

The Generalife showcases a harmonious fusion of Islamic design principles and a deep reverence for nature. The Water Stairway, lined with cascading water channels and surrounded by vibrant vegetation, exemplifies the Nasrids' mastery in creating an earthly paradise.

As you wander through these gardens, you become a part of a timeless narrative where art and nature intertwine in perfect harmony.

Alcazaba: The Fortress in Time

The Alcazaba, the oldest part of the Alhambra, stands as a sentinel overlooking Granada. This fortress, constructed for defense during times of conflict, offers a glimpse into the military prowess of the Nasrid rulers.

Ascend the Torre de la Vela to witness breathtaking views of the city, the surrounding landscape, and the distant mountains. The Alcazaba's strategic location not only provided a vantage point for defense but also served as a residence for the Nasrid rulers.

Wander through its robust walls, towers, and bastions, and let your imagination evoke the echoes of a bygone era when the Alcazaba stood as a guardian of the Nasrid dynasty. The Puerta de la Justicia, adorned with intricate inscriptions and symbols, is a testament to the Alcazaba's dual role as both a defender and a symbol of justice.

Palace of Charles V:

Amidst the Moorish splendor, the Palace of Charles V emerges as a Renaissance marvel, a testament to the evolving history of the Alhambra. Commissioned by Charles V in the 16th century, this palace presents a stark contrast to the intricate designs of the Nasrid Palaces. Its circular courtyard, surrounded by a colonnade of Doric columns, reflects Renaissance architectural principles.

Step inside to explore the palace's interior, which now houses two museums—the Museum of Fine Arts and the Museum of the Alhambra. While the Palace of Charles V represents a departure from Islamic aesthetics, it adds a layer to the Alhambra's narrative, showcasing the transition from Islamic rule to the Christian era.

Albayzín: The Historic Quarters Beyond the Walls

Venture beyond the Alhambra's walls, and you'll find yourself in the Albayzín, a historic quarter that encapsulates the essence of Granada's Moorish past.

The narrow, winding streets of the Albayzín unfold like a living labyrinth, adorned with whitewashed houses, cobblestone alleys, and vibrant markets. Explore its miradores (viewpoints) for panoramic vistas of the Alhambra, creating a dialogue between the fortress and the city it watches over.

Immerse yourself in the Albayzín's vibrant atmosphere, where the echoes of Moorish, Christian, and Jewish influences intertwine seamlessly.

Visit the Mirador de San Nicolás for an iconic view of the Alhambra against the backdrop of the Sierra Nevada mountains—a scene that encapsulates the timeless beauty of Granada.

Partal and Towers: A Waterfront to Eternity

The Partal, situated between the Generalife and the Alcazaba, offers a picturesque setting with a large reflecting pool surrounded by colonnades and gardens.

The central pavilion, framed by cypress trees, adds a touch of elegance to this waterfront sanctuary. This area allows you to appreciate the Alhambra's architectural magnificence against the tranquil backdrop of water and greenery.

Adjacent to the Partal, the Towers of the Ladies (Torres de las Damas) rise with graceful simplicity. These towers, named after

Ticketing, Entry Times, and Visitor Regulations

As you prepare to immerse yourself in this time-honored wonder, mastering the art of ticketing, understanding entry times, and adhering to visitor regulations becomes the key to unlocking its treasures seamlessly.

Securing Your Alhambra Ticket

Begin your journey into the Alhambra by acquiring the golden key—your entry ticket. In this dance with historical splendor, foresight is your trusted partner.

The demand for Alhambra tickets is as robust as its intricate architecture, so planning ahead is not just advisable but imperative. The official Alhambra website and authorized ticket vendors stand as your portals to this Moorish masterpiece.

Navigate the options gracefully, choosing the ticket that resonates with your desired exploration. Whether your heart beats in tandem with the Nasrid Palaces, craves the serenity of the Generalife Gardens, or yearns for a comprehensive Alhambra experience, your ticket becomes the overture to the enchanting symphony that awaits.

Select your time slot thoughtfully, ensuring that you secure your passage into the Nasrid Palaces—the crowning jewel of this historic realm.

Chronicles of Time: Navigating Entry Slots

In the intricate choreography of Alhambra exploration, entry times are the rhythm that guides your steps. The Nasrid Palaces, with their delicate archways and ornate chambers, operate on a scheduled entry system.

Each visitor is entrusted with a specific time slot, a moment in the narrative that guarantees an intimate dance with history, far from the cacophony of crowds.

Punctuality is your choreographer here. Align your steps with the Nasrid Palaces' designated time, ensuring a contemplative journey through its historical corridors.

Your exploration is an orchestrated ballet, and each time slot provides the rhythm that allows you to traverse the palaces with grace and unhurried contemplation.

Dawn's Elegance or Twilight's Embrace: Crafting Entry Time Poetry

The Alhambra, draped in the soft glow of dawn or bathed in the hues of twilight, offers distinct experiences depending on your chosen entry time. Early morning slots usher you into a realm of tranquility, where the Nasrid Palaces whisper tales amidst the quietude.

The gentle play of light accentuates the intricacies of the architecture, turning your morning exploration into a serene meditation.

Opting for late afternoon or evening slots grants you the privilege of witnessing the Alhambra adorned in the warm palette of sunset. As daylight fades and the Nasrid Palaces shimmer in twilight, your journey becomes a poetic dance.

Select your entry time with the discernment of an artist, aligning your experience with the atmospheric nuances of dawn or dusk, letting the Alhambra unfurl its magic in the chosen light.

Visitor Code of Conduct

Adhering to the visitor code of conduct is an essential aspect of your dance through the Alhambra. Familiarize yourself with guidelines on appropriate attire, avoiding disruptions, and respecting fellow visitors.

This code transforms your exploration into a choreographed ballet of mutual respect, creating an environment where the wonders of the Alhambra can be savored collectively while preserving its sanctity for generations to come.

Guided Tours and Audio Guides

Guided Tours:

Embarking on a guided tour through the Alhambra is akin to stepping into a living history book narrated by a knowledgeable guide. These seasoned storytellers bring the intricate details, cultural nuances, and historical significance of the Alhambra to life.

As you traverse the Nasrid Palaces, wander through the Generalife Gardens, and explore the Alcazaba fortress, a guide serves as your companion, unraveling the mysteries concealed within the walls of this UNESCO World Heritage Site.

Expert Insights:

Guides act as conduits to the past, offering a detailed narrative of the architectural marvels that define the Alhambra. They decode the symbolism embedded in the intricate arabesques, reveal the stories concealed within the Nasrid Palaces' walls, and provide historical context that transcends the physical beauty of the structures.

With each step, your understanding deepens, transforming your visit from a casual stroll to an intellectual journey through Islamic artistry.

Cultural Significance:

The Alhambra isn't just an assortment of palaces and gardens; it's a testament to the coexistence of Moorish and Spanish cultures. Guided tours act as cultural compasses, illuminating the fusion of Islamic, Christian, and Jewish influences that define the Alhambra.

Guides share stories of the Nasrid dynasty, the Reconquista, and the subsequent transformations, offering a holistic perspective that transcends the physical structures.

Navigational Grace: Maximizing Exploratio

Within the labyrinthine Alhambra, where every arch and courtyard has a story to tell, guides provide navigational prowess. They navigate you seamlessly through the Nasrid Palaces, ensuring you don't miss the delicate details of the Court of Lions or the mesmerizing views from the Alcazaba fortress. With a guide by your side, the expansive grounds become an open book, and each chapter unfolds with precision.

Audio Guides: A Personalized Symphony

If you prefer a more intimate exploration, audio guides offer a personalized journey through the Alhambra. These portable companions allow you to set your own pace, meandering through the historical nooks and crannies while absorbing information at your leisure. The Alhambra, in essence, becomes your personal stage, and the audio guide your narrator.

Flexibility of Pace:

Audio guides grant you the liberty to dictate the tempo of your journey. Whether you wish to linger in the contemplative ambiance of the Generalife Gardens or delve into the historical significance of the Alcazaba fortress, the choice is yours. The audio guide adapts to your rhythm, creating a dynamic and customized exploration experience.

Multilingual Narration: Breaking Language Barriers

The Alhambra attracts visitors from across the globe, each seeking to absorb its cultural richness. Audio guides bridge language gaps, providing multilingual narration that ensures everyone can comprehend the historical anecdotes, architectural insights, and cultural context.

This inclusivity transforms the Alhambra into a global stage, where diverse audiences can appreciate the shared heritage it embodies.

Freedom of Focus: Immersing in Personal Interests

Audio guides cater to individual interests, allowing you to focus on specific aspects of the Alhambra that resonate with you. Whether it's the intricate geometric patterns of the Nasrid Palaces, the lush greenery of the Generalife Gardens, or the strategic significance of the Alcazaba fortress, the audio guide tailors the narrative to your preferences. This freedom of focus ensures that your exploration aligns with your curiosities and passions.

Striking a Balance: Guided Tours vs. Audio Guides

Choosing between guided tours and audio guides depends on personal preferences, the depth of exploration desired, and the level of engagement sought.

Some visitors thrive on the interactive discourse provided by guides, relishing the opportunity to ask questions and engage in real-time discussions. Others prefer the autonomy and flexibility offered by audio guides, enabling them to absorb information at their own pace.

Combining Forces: The Comprehensive Experience

For a truly enriching experience, consider combining both guided tours and audio guides during your Alhambra exploration. Start with a guided tour to glean insights from a knowledgeable guide, absorbing the overarching narrative and architectural nuances.

Then, armed with an audio guide, delve deeper into specific areas of interest, allowing for a more intimate connection with the details that captivate you.

Chapter Four

Exploring Alhambra's Architectural Wonders

The Alhambra Complex: An Architectural Overview

This historic complex, recognized as a UNESCO World Heritage site, weaves together palaces, fortifications, and gardens, creating a symphony of aesthetic beauty.

At the core of the Alhambra lies the Nasrid Palaces, a series of interconnected structures that showcase the zenith of Islamic architecture. The Mexuar, the earliest section, introduces visitors to the intricate geometric patterns and elaborate stucco work that define the Nasrid style.

As you wander through the Mexuar, you'll be immersed in a world where every surface is adorned with meticulous detailing, from the ceilings to the walls, reflecting the precision and craftsmanship of the Nasrid dynasty.

Moving deeper into the complex, the Comares Palace unfolds with majestic courtyards and architectural marvels. The iconic Court of the

Myrtles, framed by a long reflecting pool, serves as a serene focal point.

The interplay of light and shadow on the intricately carved walls, embellished with Islamic calligraphy and geometric designs, creates an ethereal ambiance. It's in these spaces that one truly appreciates the marriage of art and architecture that defines the Alhambra.

The pinnacle of the Nasrid Palaces is the Palace of the Lions, a masterpiece that captures the essence of Islamic aesthetics. The central courtyard, adorned with the legendary Fountain of Lions, is a sublime example of symmetry and balance.

As you explore the palace, be prepared to be mesmerized by the muqarnas, stalactite-like arches that adorn the halls, showcasing the Nasrids' mastery of architectural intricacy. The Palace of the Lions exemplifies a harmonious blend of function and form, with each element contributing to an overall sense of splendor.

Adjacent to the palaces stands the formidable Alcazaba, a fortress that once guarded the Nasrid rulers. Climbing its towers provides not only a historical perspective but also panoramic views of Granada and the Sierra Nevada mountains.

The strategic placement of the Alcazaba within the complex highlights the Nasrids' commitment to both aesthetic beauty and practicality, ensuring a defense that mirrored the grandeur of their palaces.

Contrasting the opulence of the palaces and fortifications, the Generalife Gardens offer a serene retreat. These meticulously landscaped gardens, adorned with fountains and pools, served as a private haven for the Nasrid rulers.

The Water Stairway, a cascade of fountains, emphasizes the importance of water in Islamic art, symbolizing life and prosperity. Amidst the lush greenery, you can appreciate the delicate balance between architecture and nature that defines the Alhambra.

One cannot discuss the Alhambra without acknowledging the play of light within its walls. The ingenious use of mocárabes, intricate latticework, allows sunlight to filter through, casting enchanting patterns across the surfaces.

This interplay of light and shadow is a design element that elevates the Alhambra from a mere structure to a living canvas, captivating all who have the privilege of experiencing it.

The multicultural influences that shaped the Alhambra are evident throughout its architecture. Arab, Berber, and Christian artisans contributed to its diverse styles, creating a melting pot of artistic expression.

The Hall of the Two Sisters stands as a prime example, showcasing the fusion of Islamic and Mudejar influences in its awe-inspiring honeycomb ceiling.

To truly appreciate the Alhambra, you should plan your exploration wisely, considering the limited daily entries and the site's immense popularity. Early morning visits or off-peak seasons offer a more intimate encounter with the architectural wonders, allowing time for contemplation and admiration.

The Alcazaba: Fortress and First Line of Defense

The Alcazaba, a formidable fortress within the enchanting confines of the Alhambra, stands as both a guardian of history and a testament to mediaeval military ingenuity. As the first line of defence for the Nasrid rulers, this architectural marvel offers visitors a captivating journey through time, revealing the strategic prowess and commanding presence that characterised the Nasrid Dynasty.

Perched atop the hill with a commanding view of Granada and the Sierra Nevada, the Alcazaba served as the primary defensive structure within the Alhambra complex. Built during the mid-13th century, it reflects the Nasrid rulers' commitment to fortifying their realm against potential threats.

Approaching the Alcazaba, visitors are greeted by imposing walls, robust towers, and a sense of grandeur that befits its role as a fortress. The carefully planned defensive features, including arrow slits, battlements, and a complex system of gates, showcase the Nasrid architects' keen understanding of military architecture.

The main entrance, known as the Puerta de las Armas, welcomes visitors into the heart of the fortress. The massive wooden door, studded with iron, stands as a tangible reminder of the Alcazaba's original purpose – to safeguard the Nasrid rulers and their kingdom from external threats. As you cross the threshold, you step into a world where every stone tells a story of strategic brilliance and resilience.

Ascending through the Alcazaba's labyrinthine passages, visitors encounter the Torre del Homenaje, the central tower and crowning jewel of the fortress. This towering structure not only served as a lookout point for surveillance but also housed the living quarters of the Nasrid monarchs.

The elevated position of the Torre del Homenaje offered an unparalleled vantage point, allowing rulers to survey the landscape and monitor any approaching danger.

The strategic location of the Alcazaba within the Alhambra complex was not only about defense but also about communication. Signal towers, such as the Torre de la Vela, were strategically positioned to relay messages across the kingdom.

The lighting of fires or the use of flags could swiftly transmit vital information, enabling the Nasrid rulers to coordinate responses to potential threats.

As you explore the interior of the Alcazaba, the remnants of military structures, storage rooms, and guard chambers evoke a sense of the daily life of soldiers who once patrolled its walls.

The well-preserved cisterns and water storage systems underscore the importance of self-sufficiency, ensuring that the fortress could withstand prolonged sieges.

The architectural design of the Alcazaba also reflects a fusion of Islamic aesthetics with military functionality. Intricate decorative elements, such as geometric patterns and calligraphy, coexist with the stark pragmatism of arrow slits and defensive towers.

This harmonious blend speaks to the Nasrid Dynasty's ability to integrate beauty with purpose, creating a fortress that not only withstood physical threats but also inspired awe.

Beyond its military significance, the Alcazaba offers a captivating panorama of Granada and the surrounding landscapes. The expansive views from its walls provide a glimpse into the Nasrid rulers' strategic vision, where the fortress served not only as a shield but also as a symbolic representation of their dominance and authority.

In the shadow of the Alcazaba, visitors can sense the echoes of a bygone era when the clash of swords and the strength of fortress walls were intertwined with the tapestry of daily life.

The Alcazaba, with its rich history and architectural splendor, invites modern-day explorers to step into the shoes of Nasrid warriors and imagine the challenges and triumphs that unfolded within its formidable walls.

The Nasrid Palaces: Royal Residences of Alhambra

These royal residences, crafted during the mid-13th century, epitomize the fusion of artistic brilliance, cultural refinement, and architectural ingenuity that defined the Nasrid era.

As visitors step into the Nasrid Palaces, the Mexuar unfolds, serving as the initial chapter in the story of regal splendor. Functioning as an administrative and official space, the Mexuar exudes simplicity adorned with sophistication.

Geometric patterns, delicate stucco decorations, and intricately carved wooden ceilings weave a narrative of elegance, setting the stage for the grandeur that lies beyond.

Transitioning into the Palacio Comares, the second segment of the Nasrid Palaces, visitors encounter a realm where architectural brilliance reaches new heights. The Patio de los Arrayanes, or the Court of the Myrtles, captures the essence of Islamic paradise on earth.

A long rectangular pool surrounded by myrtle hedges reflects a meticulous integration of water and greenery, while arches and columns create a symphony of light and shadow, casting an enchanting spell upon all who enter.

Within the Palacio de Comares, the Sala de la Barca stands as a testament to Nasrid symbolism. The wooden ceiling, shaped like an inverted boat, invites contemplation of themes related to journeys and passages, further enriching the cultural narrative woven into the architecture.

The Palacio de Comares encapsulates the Nasrid rulers' ability to marry functionality with artistic expression, creating a space that harmoniously blends aesthetics and purpose.

The culmination of this regal journey unfolds in the iconic Court of the Lions, situated within the Palacio de los Leones. This breathtaking courtyard, with its central fountain supported by twelve marble lions, stands as the zenith of Nasrid craftsmanship.

The intricate interplay of water, light, and the delicate stucco decorations on surrounding galleries epitomizes the delicate balance achieved in Nasrid art and architecture.

The Court of the Lions is not merely a physical space; it is a living canvas where the Nasrid Dynasty's cultural and artistic aspirations come to life.

Journeying through the Nasrid Palaces reveals the Sala de los Abencerrajes, a space steeped in both tragedy and beauty. The domed ceiling, featuring a mesmerizing star-shaped opening, serves as a poignant reminder of a tragic event during the Nasrid period.

The narrative interwoven into the architecture adds layers of complexity, inviting visitors to not only appreciate the visual splendor but also connect with the human stories etched into the walls of these palatial halls.

Adjacent to the Court of the Lions, the Palacio de los Reyes unveils the Sala de los Reyes, adorned with a celestial-themed domed ceiling. Celestial motifs and intricate detailing underscore the Nasrid rulers' connection to higher realms, portraying a delicate equilibrium between earthly power and divine influence.

The Nasrid Palaces, in their entirety, reflect a worldview where the rulers sought to intertwine the terrestrial with the celestial, creating spaces that transcended the mundane.

The private quarters of the Nasrid rulers, known as the Harem, provide an intimate glimpse into domestic life within the palaces.

Secluded courtyards, tiled walls, ornate ceilings, and private chambers evoke the luxurious lifestyle led by the royal family. The Nasrid Palaces not only served as symbols of political authority but also as sanctuaries of comfort and leisure.

Beyond their aesthetic allure, the Nasrid Palaces showcase advanced engineering and technological marvels of their time.

The ingenious use of irrigation systems, strategic ventilation techniques, and an astute understanding of solar orientation underscore the Nasrid architects' commitment to marrying luxury with practicality.

The Generalife: Gardens and Summer Retreat

The Generalife, a verdant oasis within the storied walls of the Alhambra, beckons visitors into a realm of tranquility, beauty, and resplendent design. As the summer retreat of the Nasrid rulers, these gardens stand as a testament to the appreciation of nature, the artistry of Islamic landscape design, and the desire for a respite from the formalities of court life.

The Generalife unfolds as a paradise within a paradise. The name "Generalife" itself, derived from the Arabic "Jannat al-'Arif" or "Architect's Garden," alludes to the meticulous planning and design that characterize these enchanting gardens.

Crafted during the Nasrid Dynasty in the 14th century, the Generalife captures the essence of Islamic garden philosophy, blending aesthetics with functionality.

The journey through the Generalife commences at the Lower Gardens, a symphony of greenery and water features. Tall cypress trees and manicured hedges create a sense of order, while vibrant flowers add splashes of color to the landscape.

Meandering paths lead visitors through a series of terraces, each offering a unique perspective of the gardens and the Alhambra beyond.

Ascending through the terraces, the enchanting Patio de la Acequia reveals itself—a masterpiece of Islamic garden design. The long, central pool flanked by symmetrical beds of flowers embodies the concept of water as a life-giving element and reflects the Nasrid Dynasty's understanding of the natural world. The soothing sound of water, coupled with the scent of blossoms, creates an oasis of serenity amid the bustling energy of the Alhambra.

Moving further into the Upper Gardens, visitors encounter the Generalife Palace, the summer residence of the Nasrid rulers. The palace, characterized by its simple elegance, features courtyards, patios, and windows strategically positioned to capture the cool breezes from the surrounding hills.

The Palacio de Generalife allows guests to step into the private realm of the Nasrid monarchs, where leisure and contemplation took precedence over the formalities of court life.

One of the iconic features of the Generalife is the iconic Water Stairway, where water cascades down a series of steps, creating a dynamic and refreshing ambiance.

This ingenious water management system not only adds to the visual allure but also serves as a practical method of cooling the surroundings during the scorching summer months.

The intimate Patio de la Sultana within the Upper Gardens provides a glimpse into the Nasrid rulers' appreciation for nature and solitude. Surrounded by lush greenery, the patio features a central fountain, offering a secluded space for reflection and leisure. The design reflects the Islamic concept of the garden as a place of sensory delight and contemplation.

The Generalife's strategic location on the Hill of the Sun also bestows breathtaking panoramic views of Granada and the Alhambra. The Mirador de la Acequia, a viewpoint within the gardens, allows visitors to gaze upon the Nasrid Palaces, the Alcazaba, and the sprawling city below.

This harmonious integration of natural beauty and architectural marvels encapsulates the Nasrid rulers' vision of creating a retreat that celebrated the splendours of both man-made and natural landscapes.

Beyond its visual appeal, the Generalife embodies the principles of Islamic garden design, known as "charbagh." This ancient concept divides the garden into four quadrants, symbolising the Islamic paradise on earth.

The meticulous organisation of plants, geometric layouts, and the integration of water features reflect the Nasrid Dynasty's commitment to creating an earthly Eden within the confines of the Alhambra.

Chapter Five
The Nasrid Palaces: Jewel of Alhambra

The Court of the Myrtles: Beauty and Serenity

The Court of the Myrtles, a sublime jewel within the Nasrid Palaces of the Alhambra, unfolds as an exquisite testament to the Nasrid rulers' mastery in melding beauty and serenity.

This captivating courtyard, also known as the Patio de los Arrayanes, stands at the heart of the Palacio de Comares, capturing the essence of Islamic paradise on earth through its meticulously designed elements.

As you step into the Court of the Myrtles, a scene of unrivaled elegance unfolds. The courtyard's name, derived from the myrtle hedges lining the long rectangular pool, conjures images of lush greenery that interplays with the cool, reflective waters.

This central pool, mirroring the surrounding architectural splendours, creates a harmonious balance between the built environment and the natural world—a hallmark of Nasrid aesthetic philosophy.

The design of the Court of the Myrtles embodies the Nasrid rulers' deep appreciation for symmetry and geometric precision. The long pool, flanked by pristine myrtle hedges, serves as the focal point, drawing the eye towards the intricate details of the surrounding architecture.

The linear arrangement of galleries, columns, and arches showcases the Nasrid Dynasty's commitment to creating visual harmony within the confines of the Alhambra.

The surrounding galleries, adorned with delicately carved columns and arches, elevate the Court of the Myrtles to an aesthetic masterpiece. The interplay of light and shadow within these galleries adds a dynamic quality to the space, transforming its ambiance throughout the day.

As sunlight dances upon the intricate stucco decorations, the courtyard becomes a canvas where time appears to stand still, inviting contemplation and appreciation.

The Nasrid rulers' attention to water features within the Alhambra reaches its zenith in the Court of the Myrtles. The long pool not only serves an aesthetic purpose but also embodies the Nasrid concept of water as a life-giving element, a source of serenity, and a reflection of paradise.

The tranquil sounds of water, combined with the fragrant myrtle hedges, create an immersive sensory experience that transports visitors into an oasis of calm within the bustling palace.

As visitors stroll along the galleries surrounding the Court of the Myrtles, they encounter the Patio de los Gomérez, a small garden area named after the Gomérez family, who were the last Moors allowed to reside in the Alhambra after the Christian conquest.

This intimate space, adorned with orange trees and other vegetation, offers a contemplative respite within the larger courtyard. The juxtaposition of nature with the architectural elements emphasizes the Nasrid rulers' dedication to creating holistic and harmonious environments.

The Court of the Myrtles is not merely a visual spectacle; it carries historical echoes and narratives within its finely crafted walls. It served as a stage for various ceremonies, receptions, and official events during the Nasrid period.

The courtyard witnessed the ebb and flow of court life, the echo of footsteps across its marble floors, and the exchange of ideas and cultural expressions within its serene embrace.

One of the most captivating features of the Court of the Myrtles is the Torre de Comares, a tower that overlooks the courtyard. This tower, with its intricate facade and commanding presence, not only adds to the visual grandeur of the space but also serves as a vantage point for the Nasrid rulers to observe the events unfolding below.

The Torre de Comares, with its elegant design, embodies the Nasrid Dynasty's commitment to merging architectural beauty with strategic functionality.

The Palace of the Lions: A Masterpiece of Islamic Art

The Palace of the Lions, an exquisite jewel within the Nasrid Palaces of the Alhambra, stands as a crowning achievement of Islamic art and architectural brilliance. Crafted during the mid-14th century, this masterpiece reflects the Nasrid rulers' commitment to creating spaces that seamlessly blended aesthetics, functionality, and spiritual symbolism.

As visitors step into the Palace of the Lions, they are welcomed into a realm of unparalleled beauty and intricate craftsmanship. The name itself evokes a sense of regality, derived from the iconic central courtyard adorned with a fountain supported by twelve marble lions—a breathtaking centrepiece that captures the essence of Nasrid artistry.

The heart of the Palace of the Lions is the iconic Court of the Lions, or Patio de los Leones, a sublime space where geometric precision and artistic finesse converge. The central fountain, supported by twelve majestic lions, symbolises strength, courage, and power—the very qualities attributed to the Nasrid Dynasty.

The arrangement of the lions, each spouting water towards the centre, creates a mesmerising symphony of water that both cools the space and serves as a visual metaphor for the interconnectedness of life.

Surrounding the Court of the Lions, the galleries adorned with delicate columns and horseshoe arches showcase the Nasrid architects' mastery in Islamic geometric patterns and calligraphy.

The intricately carved stucco decorations that embellish the arches and walls are a testament to the Nasrid Dynasty's commitment to transforming the palace into a living canvas, where every inch exudes aesthetic refinement.

The ingenious water management system within the Palace of the Lions further elevates its status as a masterpiece of engineering. A sophisticated network of pipes concealed beneath the marble flooring channels water to various parts of the palace, facilitating both decorative fountains and practical irrigation for the gardens.

This harmonious integration of form and function attests to the Nasrid rulers' advanced understanding of hydraulics and their desire to create an environment that celebrated the beauty and sound of water.

The Hall of the Abencerrajes within the Palace of the Lions adds a layer of historical intrigue to the architectural splendor. The hall features a domed ceiling adorned with an exquisite star-shaped opening, creating an ethereal play of light.

According to legend, this hall witnessed a tragic event during the Nasrid period—the beheading of members of the Abencerrajes noble family. This story, though tinged with sorrow, contributes to the mystique and narrative depth of the Palace of the Lions.

Adjacent to the Court of the Lions, the Hall of the Two Sisters (Sala de Dos Hermanas) captivates with its stunning honeycomb Muqarnas vault. The intricate stalactite-like structures that adorn the ceiling showcase the Nasrid architects' skill in creating visually stunning yet structurally sound designs.

The delicate interplay of light and shadow within this hall enhances its ethereal quality, inviting visitors into a space where art and architecture seamlessly merge.

The Nasrid rulers' dedication to spiritual symbolism is evident in the Mihrab, a niche indicating the direction of Mecca, located within the Palace of the Lions. This sacred element serves as a focal point, underscoring the Nasrid Dynasty's commitment to infusing their royal abode with a spiritual dimension.

The Mihrab's embellishments, including Quranic inscriptions and intricate patterns, elevate it beyond a mere architectural feature, transforming it into a spiritual centerpiece within the palace.

The residential quarters of the Palace of the Lions also feature private chambers, courtyards, and additional spaces that showcase the Nasrid rulers' penchant for luxury and comfort.

The integration of courtyards with rooms, known as a "Casa Patio," allows for natural ventilation and privacy, reflecting the Nasrid Dynasty's understanding of practicality and aesthetics in residential design.

The Palace of Charles V: The Blend of Christian and Islamic Styles

The Palace of Charles V, an intriguing architectural gem situated beautifully of the Alhambra, stands as a testament to the interplay of history, culture, and artistic vision.

Commissioned by Emperor Charles V in the 16th century, this palace represents a unique fusion of Christian and Islamic architectural styles, creating a harmonious dialogue between two distinct cultural epochs.

Constructed within the Nasrid Palaces, the Palace of Charles V emerges as a striking departure from the intricate ornamentation and geometric precision that characterize its surroundings.

The imposing structure, with its monumental proportions and Renaissance-inspired design, reflects the Emperor's desire to leave an indelible mark on the Alhambra, connecting it with the evolving aesthetics of the European Renaissance.

As visitors approach the Palace of Charles V, the transition from the Nasrid architecture to the Renaissance grandeur is immediately apparent. The colossal circular courtyard at the center of the palace, known as the Patio Oval, serves as a grand forecourt, juxtaposing the symmetrical gardens and courtyards of the Nasrid Palaces.

This deliberate departure from Islamic design principles signifies the embrace of Renaissance ideals, mirroring the emperor's cultural and political ambitions.

The commanding exterior of the palace, with its austere yet elegant facade, exemplifies classical Renaissance elements such as pilasters, columns, and geometric patterns. The contrast between the simplicity of the exterior and the intricacy of the Nasrid Palaces surrounding it creates a visual dialogue, inviting contemplation on the intersection of two rich cultural heritages.

Stepping inside the Palace of Charles V, visitors encounter a central circular courtyard surrounded by two levels of colonnades. The architectural harmony of the courtyard, echoing the proportions of ancient Roman buildings, pays homage to classical ideals while departing from the intricate layouts of Islamic architecture.

This intentional blend serves as a metaphor for the merging of diverse cultures and signifies the transitional period in which the palace was conceived.

The upper level of the palace houses the Museo de Bellas Artes (Museum of Fine Arts), adding yet another layer of cultural significance. The museum showcases an impressive collection of Spanish Renaissance and Baroque art, providing visitors with an opportunity to appreciate the evolution of artistic expression from the medieval to the modern era. The juxtaposition of these artworks within the Renaissance-inspired structure reinforces the interweaving of historical narratives and artistic styles.

The Palacio de Carlos V, an architectural masterpiece within the palace complex, features a circular hall adorned with a stunning dome. The dome, reminiscent of Renaissance domes in Italy, reflects the architectural influence of Filippo Brunelleschi's pioneering designs.

This central space serves as a testament to the exchange of ideas and artistic innovation that characterized the Renaissance era, transcending geographical and cultural boundaries.

While the Palace of Charles V is primarily characterized by its departure from Islamic aesthetics, there are subtle nods to the Alhambra's Moorish heritage.

The use of horseshoe arches in certain sections of the palace pays homage to Islamic architectural elements, creating a sense of continuity with the Nasrid legacy. This intentional incorporation serves as a bridge between the two distinct architectural languages, showcasing the Emperor's appreciation for the rich cultural tapestry of the Alhambra.

The surrounding gardens, known as the Jardines del Generalife, also reflect the fusion of European and Moorish landscaping traditions. The geometric layout and symmetrical patterns echo Renaissance garden design, while the use of water features and terraced landscapes pays homage to the water-centric gardens of the Nasrid era. This harmonious coexistence of influences transforms the gardens into a tranquil space that encapsulates the shared history of the Alhambra.

Chapter Six
Discovering Alhambra's Cultural Heritage

Alhambra's Cultural Significance: A Tapestry of Influences

This iconic fortress, with its intricate palaces, lush gardens, and commanding views, weaves a rich tapestry of influences that reflect the diverse historical, artistic, and philosophical currents that have shaped its character.

At the heart of the Alhambra's cultural significance lies its Moorish heritage. Constructed during the Nasrid Dynasty's reign from the 13th to the 15th centuries, the palace complex embodies the zenith of Islamic art and architecture.

The Nasrid Palaces, with their intricate geometric patterns, horseshoe arches, and calligraphic inscriptions, showcase the sophisticated aesthetic sensibilities of Islamic civilization. The intricate stucco decorations, arabesque motifs, and poetic inscriptions that adorn the walls evoke a sense of transcendent beauty, capturing the essence of Islamic art.

The Alhambra also serves as a testament to the Islamic approach to gardens as places of paradise on earth. The Generalife, the summer retreat of the Nasrid rulers, features lush greenery, fragrant flowers, and intricately designed water features.

The concept of "charbagh," a Persian-inspired quadrilateral garden layout, is manifested in the symmetrically arranged terraces and water channels, creating a serene and harmonious environment.

However, the cultural tapestry of the Alhambra is not confined to Islamic influences alone. The conquest of Granada by the Catholic Monarchs Ferdinand and Isabella in 1492 ushered in a new chapter in the site's history. The subsequent construction of the Palace of Charles V within the Alhambra complex marks the fusion of Christian and Islamic architectural styles.

The imposing Renaissance structure, with its circular courtyard and classical columns, provides a stark contrast to the intricate designs of the Nasrid Palaces, showcasing the evolving cultural landscape during the 16th century.

The synthesis of Christian and Islamic elements within the Alhambra is further evident in the Alcazaba, the fortress portion of the complex.

With its defensive walls, towers, and military structures, the Alcazaba reflects the military engineering of the Islamic period.

However, subsequent additions, including the Gate of Justice with its Christian-style triumphal arch, reveal the transformative impact of the Reconquista on the Alhambra's cultural identity.

The Alhambra also echoes the Mudejar architectural tradition, a style that emerged in the Iberian Peninsula when Islamic craftsmen continued to work under Christian rule. The intricate wooden ceilings, colorful tiles, and detailed plasterwork found in various parts of the complex illustrate the enduring influence of Mudejar craftsmanship.

These elements bear witness to the cross-cultural exchange that characterized the post-Reconquista era, illustrating how Islamic artistic traditions persisted and blended with emerging Christian influences.

Beyond architecture, the Alhambra's cultural significance extends to its literary heritage. The palace complex is adorned with inscriptions of poetry and philosophical musings, reflecting the intellectual vibrancy of the Nasrid court.

These inscriptions not only showcase the importance of literature in Nasrid culture but also emphasize the interconnectedness of artistic and intellectual pursuits within the Alhambra's walls.

The Alhambra's impact on literature extends beyond its own time. The allure of the palace complex has inspired writers and poets over the centuries, contributing to the development of the Orientalist movement in the 19th century.

The romantic fascination with the Alhambra, exemplified by Washington Irving's "Tales of the Alhambra," played a crucial role in shaping Western perceptions of the Islamic world and influencing subsequent artistic and literary works.

In the realm of music, the Alhambra's cultural resonance is evident in compositions that draw inspiration from its mystical ambiance. Musicians and composers have sought to capture the spirit of the Alhambra through melodies that evoke the grandeur, beauty, and historical richness of the site. This musical legacy serves as an auditory tribute to the Alhambra's enduring cultural significance.

Islamic Art and Architecture in Alhambra

The Alhambra, emerges as a peerless masterpiece of Islamic art and architecture, a living testament to the rich cultural heritage of the Nasrid Dynasty.

Crafted during the 13th to 15th centuries, the Nasrid Palaces within the Alhambra encapsulate the zenith of Islamic civilization, reflecting an unparalleled fusion of aesthetics, innovation, and cultural refinement.

At the heart of the Alhambra's Islamic artistry lies a profound appreciation for geometric precision. The Nasrid Palaces are adorned with an intricate mosaic of geometric patterns, exemplified in the exquisite tilework, stucco carvings, and wooden ceilings.

These geometric designs, often based on complex mathematical principles, create a mesmerizing visual symphony that permeates every corner of the Alhambra. The Alhambra's geometric motifs are not merely decorative but serve as a symbolic expression of the divine order and harmony that underlie the Islamic worldview.

One of the defining features of Islamic architecture within the Alhambra is the ubiquitous use of horseshoe arches. These graceful arches, characterized by their rounded shape, are prominent in the Nasrid Palaces, creating a sense of elegance and rhythm.

The arches are not merely structural elements but also serve symbolic purposes, evoking the idea of continuity and infinity—a visual representation of the boundless nature of divine beauty.

The art of calligraphy, a revered form of expression in Islamic culture, is lavishly displayed throughout the Alhambra. Inscriptions from Arabic poetry, verses from the Quran, and Nasrid mottos adorn the walls, arches, and courtyards.

The calligraphy, often rendered in intricate scripts, becomes an integral part of the architectural design, transforming the Alhambra into a repository of literary and spiritual wisdom. These inscriptions not only elevate the aesthetic beauty of the palaces but also invite contemplation, connecting visitors with the cultural and intellectual currents of the Nasrid period.

The interplay of light and shadow within the Alhambra is another hallmark of Islamic architectural ingenuity. The lattice-like screens, known as "mashrabiya" or "jali," filter sunlight into delicate patterns that dance across the surfaces of the Nasrid Palaces.

This play of light not only adds a dynamic quality to the visual experience but also reflects the Islamic concept of light as a metaphor for divine guidance. The Alhambra's ingenious use of light and shadow creates an ever-changing ambiance that enhances the spiritual and aesthetic dimensions of its architecture.

Water, revered as a symbol of life and purity in Islamic culture, takes center stage in the Alhambra's design. The complex features an intricate network of fountains, pools, and channels, culminating in the iconic Court of the Lions.

The central fountain in this court, supported by twelve marble lions, symbolizes strength and regality while also serving a practical purpose of providing a soothing soundscape. Water not only cools the environment but also amplifies the sensory experience, enveloping visitors in a multisensory journey through the Nasrid Palaces.

The Nasrid architects' astute understanding of the surrounding landscape is evident in the strategic placement of windows and courtyards, framing breathtaking views of Granada and the surrounding mountains.

This integration of the natural environment into the architectural design aligns with the Islamic principle of "fitra," emphasizing the inherent connection between human beings and nature.

The Nasrid Palaces also exhibit the ingenious use of "muqarnas," intricate honeycomb-like structures that embellish the ceilings. These stalactite-like formations, aside from their aesthetic appeal, serve both structural and acoustical purposes.

The muqarnas exemplify the Nasrid architects' ability to merge beauty with functionality, creating spaces that are not only visually stunning but also technologically advanced for their time.

The Alhambra's Nasrid Palaces are replete with intimate courtyards, such as the Patio de los Leones and the Patio de los Arrayanes, each a unique expression of Islamic garden design principles.

The harmonious integration of water features, greenery, and architectural elements within these courtyards reflects the Islamic concept of paradise on earth, providing tranquil havens for contemplation and leisure.

Moorish Influence on Spanish Culture

The enduring legacy of Moorish influence on Spanish culture is a captivating journey through time, tracing back to the medieval era when Islamic rule left an indelible mark on the Iberian Peninsula. Nowhere is this influence more palpable and enchanting than in the Alhambra, the crowning jewel of Moorish architecture, and its echoes reverberate through the fabric of Spain's cultural tapestry.

The Alhambra, constructed during the Nasrid Dynasty's rule from the 13th to the 15th centuries, stands as a testament to the brilliance of Moorish architectural and artistic achievements.

This fortress-palace, with its intricate geometric patterns, horseshoe arches, and luscious gardens, embodies the quintessence of Moorish design principles. The Alhambra is a living testament to the synthesis of diverse cultural influences, reflecting the intricate dance between Islamic, Christian, and Jewish traditions that characterized medieval Iberia.

One of the most distinctive features of Moorish architecture that permeates Spanish culture is the horseshoe arch. The graceful curve of this arch, found abundantly throughout the Alhambra, became an enduring motif in Spanish architecture.

It found its way into cathedrals, synagogues, and palaces across Spain, serving as a tangible reminder of the Moorish craftsmanship that once graced the Iberian Peninsula. This architectural legacy stands as a bridge between Islamic and European styles, contributing to the unique blend that defines Spanish cultural identity.

The Alhambra's intricate tilework, known as "azulejos," is another hallmark of Moorish influence that has left an indelible imprint on Spanish aesthetics. These vibrant, geometrically patterned ceramic tiles, adorning walls, floors, and ceilings within the Nasrid Palaces, have become emblematic of Moorish artistry.

The tradition of azulejos flourished and evolved over centuries, becoming a defining element in Spanish decorative arts, from the intricate facades of Seville's Alcázar to the charming interiors of Andalusian homes.

Moorish influence extends beyond architectural aesthetics into the realm of language, as Arabic left an enduring imprint on the Spanish lexicon.

The Arabic language, with its poetic richness, bestowed upon Spanish a wealth of vocabulary that permeates everyday speech. Words like "aceituna" (olive), "azúcar" (sugar), and "alcohol" bear witness to the linguistic legacy of Moorish rule, offering a linguistic tapestry that enriches the Spanish language.

The culinary landscape of Spain also bears the unmistakable stamp of Moorish influence, particularly in the southern regions of Andalusia.

The introduction of ingredients such as almonds, rice, and spices transformed the culinary traditions of the Iberian Peninsula. Iconic dishes like paella, with its aromatic blend of saffron-infused rice and diverse ingredients, reflect the Moorish culinary legacy that continues to tantalize taste buds across Spain.

Moorish influence on Spanish music is evident in the melodic echoes of Andalusian flamenco, a genre deeply rooted in the region's cultural history. The intricate rhythms, passionate vocals, and expressive dance movements resonate with the emotional intensity characteristic of Moorish musical traditions. The haunting strains of the flamenco guitar, with its intricate fingerpicking techniques, trace their lineage back to the musical innovations of Andalusian Moors.

In the realm of science, medicine, and philosophy, Moorish contributions during the medieval period laid the groundwork for the European Renaissance. The translation movement in Toledo, where Islamic scholars translated Greek and Roman texts into Arabic, preserved and expanded upon classical knowledge. The works of Moorish philosophers like Averroes and Avicenna influenced European scholars and paved the way for the intellectual blossoming of the Renaissance.

The concept of the "patio" or inner courtyard, integral to Spanish architecture, owes its origins to the Moorish al-Andalus. The Alhambra's enchanting courtyards, such as the Court of the Lions and the Generalife gardens, served as paradigms of serene, open spaces that blurred the lines between indoors and outdoors. This architectural innovation, celebrated for its ability to provide both cooling and contemplative spaces, became a hallmark of Spanish residential design.

In literature, the impact of Moorish storytelling traditions resonates through the works of Spanish writers. The influence of One Thousand and One Nights, a collection of Middle Eastern folk tales, is particularly notable. The concept of magical realism, prevalent in the works of Spanish authors like García Márquez, finds its roots in the fantastical narratives that captivated the imagination of Moorish storytellers.

The enduring fascination with Moorish history and culture is also evident in Spain's vibrant festivals and celebrations. Events like the Feria de Abril in Seville, with its vibrant colors, lively music, and exuberant dance, echo the spirit of Andalusian fiestas influenced by Moorish traditions. The lively procession of the Moors and Christians, commemorating the historical interactions between these cultures, is a poignant illustration of Spain's complex cultural mosaic.

UNESCO World Heritage Status and Preservation Efforts

The Alhambra, a testament to the fusion of Islamic, Christian, and Mudejar influences, has earned its place on the prestigious list of UNESCO World Heritage Sites.

This designation not only recognizes the cultural and historical significance of the Alhambra but also underscores the responsibility to preserve and protect this architectural marvel for future generations.

The UNESCO World Heritage status bestowed upon the Alhambra in 1984 reflects its outstanding universal value. The Alhambra stands as a symbol of the rich tapestry of human history, a meeting point of diverse cultural traditions that coalesced in the heart of Andalusia. Its inclusion on the list recognizes the Alhambra's role in shaping the course of artistic, architectural, and intellectual evolution in the Mediterranean region.

The Alhambra, with its Nasrid Palaces, Generalife gardens, and Alcazaba fortress, encapsulates the peak of Moorish civilization. The intricate stucco decorations, horseshoe arches, calligraphic inscriptions, and serene courtyards collectively weave a narrative that transcends time. UNESCO acknowledges the Alhambra as a masterpiece of Islamic art and architecture, a living testament to the ingenuity of the Nasrid Dynasty and the cultural synthesis that defined al-Andalus.

The designation as a UNESCO World Heritage Site comes with a profound responsibility—to ensure the preservation of the Alhambra's integrity and authenticity. The site's cultural significance necessitates a delicate balance between conservation efforts and the need to make this historical treasure accessible to the public.

Preservation efforts at the Alhambra are multifaceted and comprehensive, addressing both the tangible and intangible aspects of its cultural heritage. A meticulous restoration process has been underway to safeguard the architectural elements, intricate decorations, and delicate structures that define the Nasrid Palaces.

Conservationists employ advanced technologies and traditional craftsmanship to restore and protect the Alhambra's unique features, ensuring that they retain their original beauty and historical context.

Beyond physical restoration, conservation efforts extend to managing the environmental impact on the site. The delicate balance of water features, gardens, and architectural elements requires ongoing attention to maintain the Alhambra's atmospheric and aesthetic qualities.

Sustainable practices are implemented to ensure that the site's natural and built components harmonize seamlessly, preserving the ambiance that has captivated visitors for centuries.

Visitor management is a crucial aspect of preserving the Alhambra's integrity. A delicate balance is struck between allowing access to this cultural treasure and minimizing the impact of tourism on its fragile structures.

Timed entry systems, visitor quotas, and guided tours help to protect the site from overcrowding, ensuring that each visitor can appreciate the Alhambra without compromising its preservation.

Education and public awareness initiatives play a pivotal role in the preservation efforts at the Alhambra. Programs are designed to inform visitors about the historical, cultural, and architectural significance of the site.

Understanding fosters appreciation, and an informed public becomes a collective guardian of the Alhambra's heritage. These initiatives extend to local communities, fostering a sense of shared responsibility for the preservation of this cultural gem.

Collaboration between international organizations, local authorities, and cultural institutions enhances the Alhambra's preservation efforts. Knowledge exchange, technological advancements, and best practices are shared to ensure that the Alhambra remains a beacon of cultural heritage conservation on a global scale. This collaborative approach acknowledges the interconnectedness of the world's cultural treasures and the shared responsibility to protect them.

The Alhambra, as a UNESCO World Heritage Site, is not frozen in time. Preservation efforts recognize the dynamic nature of cultural heritage and the need for adaptive strategies to address evolving challenges.

Research and documentation initiatives are ongoing to deepen the understanding of the

Alhambra's history, architecture, and cultural significance. This continuous exploration informs conservation strategies, ensuring that preservation practices remain at the forefront of cultural heritage management.

Chapter Seven

The Alhambra Museum: Treasures from the Past

The Museum's Collections and Exhibits

The Alhambra Museum stands as a captivating repository of treasures from the past, offering visitors a journey through the rich tapestry of history, art, and cultural exchange.

With its diverse collections and carefully curated exhibits, the museum provides a unique lens through which to explore the layered heritage of this iconic fortress-palace.

The museum's collections, spanning various periods and cultural influences, serve as a bridge between the Islamic, Christian, and Mudejar epochs that have left an indelible mark on the Alhambra.

As visitors traverse its halls, they encounter a curated narrative that unfolds through artifacts, manuscripts, and artworks, unveiling the multifaceted history of this architectural gem.

One of the museum's highlights is the collection of Nasrid artifacts, transporting visitors back to the zenith of Islamic rule in the Iberian Peninsula. Delicate ceramic tiles, intricately carved stucco panels, and fragments of exquisite calligraphy showcase the unparalleled craftsmanship of the Nasrid artisans.

These artifacts, once integral to the Nasrid Palaces, are now preserved within the museum, allowing visitors to witness the refinement and artistry that defined the Nasrid Dynasty's cultural legacy.

The Nasrid Palaces are also represented through scale models and reconstructions within the museum, offering a three-dimensional insight into the architectural brilliance of structures such as the Court of the Lions, the Hall of the Abencerrajes, and the Hall of the Ambassadors.

These detailed representations bring to life the grandeur of the Nasrid era, allowing visitors to appreciate the intricate designs and spatial dynamics of the palaces.

As the narrative unfolds, the museum seamlessly transitions into the Christian era, marked by the conquest of Granada in 1492. Artifacts and objects from this period, including Christian artworks, liturgical items, and architectural elements, illustrate the transformation of the

Alhambra from a Muslim stronghold to a symbol of Christian power.

The juxtaposition of these artifacts echoes the complex interplay of cultures and religions that characterized the Alhambra's history.

The museum's exhibits also delve into the Mudejar influence on the Alhambra, showcasing the continuation of Islamic artistic traditions under Christian rule. Mudejar craftsmanship is evident in wooden ceilings, colorful tiles, and decorative elements that seamlessly blend Islamic and Christian motifs.

This section of the museum provides a nuanced understanding of how cultural exchange and artistic collaboration persisted even during times of political and religious change.

One of the museum's crown jewels is the collection of illuminated manuscripts, showcasing the intellectual and artistic achievements of al-Andalus. Manuscripts featuring Arabic calligraphy, geometric patterns, and illustrations highlight the rich literary and scientific heritage of the region.

These beautifully crafted manuscripts provide insights into the intellectual pursuits that flourished within the Nasrid court and contribute to a deeper appreciation of the cultural vibrancy of medieval al-Andalus.

The Alhambra Museum doesn't merely focus on the distant past; it also explores the 19th-century romantic fascination with the Alhambra. Visitors encounter artifacts, paintings, and memorabilia from this period, including works inspired by Washington Irving's "Tales of the Alhambra."

This section of the museum sheds light on how the Alhambra captured the imagination of writers, artists, and travelers during the Romantic era, contributing to the site's enduring allure.

The museum also employs multimedia installations and interactive displays to enhance the visitor experience. Audiovisual presentations bring historical narratives to life, allowing visitors to immerse themselves in the sounds, colors, and stories of the Alhambra.

These dynamic elements serve to create a more engaging and educational journey through the cultural heritage preserved within the museum's walls.

The Alhambra Museum's commitment to education extends beyond its exhibits. It hosts lectures, workshops, and educational programs that cater to diverse audiences, from scholars to schoolchildren.

These initiatives aim to foster a deeper understanding of the Alhambra's historical, artistic, and cultural significance, ensuring that its legacy resonates with present and future generations.

The museum's dedication to preservation and scholarship is evident in ongoing research and conservation efforts. Collaborations with international institutions, scholars, and experts contribute to the continuous refinement and expansion of the museum's collections.

This commitment to scholarly excellence ensures that the Alhambra Museum remains at the forefront of cultural heritage conservation and interpretation.

Notable Artefacts and Historical Objects

Within the hallowed halls of the Alhambra Museum, an extraordinary array of artifacts and historical objects awaits, each telling a unique tale of the illustrious past that unfolded within the walls of this iconic fortress-palace.

These treasures, carefully curated and displayed, serve as tangible links to the diverse cultures and epochs that have shaped the Alhambra's rich heritage.

One of the most notable artifacts housed within the museum is the intricately carved wooden mihrab from the Mosque of the Alhambra. This mihrab, a niche indicating the direction of Mecca, is a testament to the spiritual and artistic prowess of the Nasrid artisans.

Adorned with geometric patterns, calligraphic inscriptions, and delicate arabesques, the mihrab stands as a masterpiece of Islamic craftsmanship, embodying the reverence and devotion that permeated the Nasrid era.

The museum's collection also boasts a remarkable selection of Nasrid ceramic tiles, providing a glimpse into the sophisticated tilework that adorned the Nasrid Palaces.

These tiles, adorned with geometric motifs, stylized floral patterns, and intricate calligraphy, reflect the Nasrid Dynasty's commitment to elevating everyday surfaces into works of art. Each tile tells a story, narrating the aesthetics and cultural nuances of medieval al-Andalus.

As visitors explore the exhibits, they encounter fragments of stucco decorations that once graced the Nasrid Palaces. These fragments, intricately carved with geometric and vegetal motifs, offer insights into the architectural splendor that characterized the Nasrid architectural language.

The delicate nature of the stucco carvings speaks to the Nasrid artisans' mastery in transforming plaster into ethereal works of art, creating an otherworldly ambiance within the palace walls.

The Alhambra Museum provides a fascinating glimpse into the Nasrid court's literary pursuits with its collection of illuminated manuscripts. One such manuscript, showcasing Arabic calligraphy and vibrant illustrations, exemplifies the intellectual vibrancy that characterized the Nasrid era.

These manuscripts, often containing works of poetry, philosophy, and science, underscore the multifaceted cultural legacy of the Nasrid Dynasty.

The transition to the Christian era is marked by a collection of artifacts that reflect the transformation of the Alhambra after the Reconquista. Ecclesiastical objects, Christian artworks, and liturgical items illustrate the adaptation of the site to its new role within the Christian kingdom.

A notable artifact is a Christian altarpiece, a visual representation of the cultural amalgamation that unfolded within the Alhambra's walls during this historical transition.

Mudejar influence, a unique blend of Islamic and Christian artistic elements, is palpable in the museum's collection of wooden ceilings. These intricately carved masterpieces showcase the continuation of Islamic craftsmanship under Christian rule.

The delicate interplay of geometric patterns, arabesques, and Christian symbols in the wooden ceilings exemplifies the harmonious coexistence of diverse cultural influences within the Alhambra.

One of the most iconic objects in the museum is the "Alhambra Vase," an exquisite piece of Nasrid ceramics. This intricately decorated vase, adorned with geometric patterns and poetic inscriptions, epitomizes the Nasrid Dynasty's mastery in ceramic arts. The Alhambra Vase serves as a symbol of the fusion of art and craftsmanship that defined the Nasrid era, captivating the imagination of visitors with its timeless elegance.

The museum's collection extends beyond physical artifacts to include architectural models and reconstructions that offer a holistic understanding of the Nasrid Palaces. Scale models of key architectural elements, such as the Court of the Lions and the Hall of the Abencerrajes, provide a three-dimensional exploration of the Nasrid architectural brilliance.

These reconstructions offer visitors a virtual journey through the palaces, allowing them to appreciate the spatial dynamics and intricate details of these architectural wonders.

The Alhambra Museum pays homage to the 19th-century Romantic era with its collection of artworks inspired by Washington Irving's "Tales of the Alhambra." Paintings, illustrations, and memorabilia from this period capture the romantic fascination that the Alhambra evoked in the imaginations of artists and writers.

These artifacts transport visitors to a time when the Alhambra became a source of inspiration for the Romantic movement, contributing to its enduring allure.

The museum also houses objects and artifacts that shed light on the daily life within the Alhambra, including items of domestic use, tools, and utensils. These artifacts provide a glimpse into the practical aspects of life during different historical periods, offering a more nuanced understanding of the diverse communities that inhabited the Alhambra over the centuries.

Multimedia installations within the museum complement the static exhibits, enriching the visitor experience. Audiovisual presentations, interactive displays, and immersive technologies bring historical narratives to life, creating a dynamic and engaging exploration of the Alhambra's cultural heritage.

These multimedia elements serve as a bridge between the past and the present, inviting visitors to interact with the artifacts and delve deeper into the stories they tell.

Exploring the Museum's Interactive Displays

The Alhambra Museum transcends traditional exhibits with its innovative and interactive displays. As explorers step into this cultural haven within the Alhambra's walls, they are greeted by a dynamic blend of technology, storytelling, and historical artefacts that breathe life into the rich tapestry of the past.

One of the museum's standout interactive features is the augmented reality (AR) experience that brings architectural elements to life. As visitors hold up devices equipped with AR technology, they witness the resurrection of Nasrid Palaces' key structures.

The Court of the Lions, the Hall of the Abencerrajes, and other architectural marvels materialize in three-dimensional splendor, allowing visitors to virtually stroll through the palaces and marvel at the intricacies of Nasrid craftsmanship.

This interactive display provides a visceral connection to the architectural brilliance of the past, inviting visitors to explore the Alhambra in a way that transcends conventional boundaries.

Touchscreen displays strategically positioned throughout the museum offer an interactive portal to the Alhambra's diverse cultural influences. These displays allow visitors to navigate through the history of the Nasrid Dynasty, Christian conquest, and Mudejar period with a mere swipe of their fingertips.

Rich multimedia content, including images, videos, and historical narratives, unfolds seamlessly, providing a comprehensive understanding of the multifaceted heritage enshrined within the Alhambra.

A particularly captivating interactive feature is the "Time Traveler's Guide," an augmented reality application that overlays historical images onto the current museum space.

Visitors equipped with compatible devices can witness the evolution of the Alhambra, from its Nasrid splendor to its Christian transformations, superimposed on the actual surroundings. This technological marvel allows for a captivating juxtaposition of past and present, offering a visual narrative that transcends the confines of traditional museum exhibits.

The museum's touchscreen tables serve as interactive hubs where visitors can delve deeper into specific artifacts and historical periods. These tables offer a tactile exploration of Nasrid ceramics, Christian liturgical items, Mudejar wooden ceilings, and other treasures.

With a simple touch, visitors can access detailed information, zoom in on intricate details, and uncover the stories behind each artifact. This hands-on approach transforms the museum experience into an engaging and personalized exploration of the Alhambra's cultural heritage.

If you seek a multisensory immersion, the museum incorporates interactive soundscapes that complement various exhibits. As visitors approach Nasrid artifacts, the ambient sounds of flowing water, distant echoes of poetry, and the soft rustle of leaves in the Generalife gardens create an evocative atmosphere.

These immersive soundscapes transport visitors to the historical contexts of the Nasrid era, providing a sensory journey that enhances the overall museum experience.

The Alhambra Museum's commitment to inclusivity and accessibility is evident in its incorporation of tactile displays. Specially designed for visitors with visual impairments, these tactile exhibits allow individuals to explore replicas of key artifacts through touch.

Braille descriptions accompany each tactile display, ensuring that visitors with visual disabilities can engage with the museum's collections independently. This thoughtful integration of tactile elements fosters a more inclusive and enriching experience for all visitors.

Augmented reality storytelling takes center stage in the museum's dedicated narrative spaces. Here, visitors don AR glasses that transport them into historical vignettes, where Nasrid rulers, Christian conquerors, and Mudejar artisans come to life.

These interactive narratives unfold in the very spaces where historical events transpired, creating a seamless integration of technology and physical environment. Visitors become active participants in the unfolding drama of the Alhambra's history, experiencing pivotal moments through a captivating blend of virtual and real-world elements.

The Alhambra Museum's commitment to educational outreach is reflected in its interactive learning stations. Designed for school groups and curious minds of all ages, these stations offer hands-on activities, quizzes, and games that make learning about the Alhambra's history an engaging adventure.

From building miniature Nasrid arches to solving historical puzzles, these interactive learning experiences cater to diverse learning styles and foster a sense of discovery.

The museum's virtual reality (VR) exhibits provide a cutting-edge exploration of the Alhambra's architectural wonders. Equipped with VR headsets, visitors can virtually step into the Nasrid Palaces, wander through the Generalife gardens, and stand atop the Alcazaba fortress.

This immersive experience transcends the limitations of physical space, offering an unparalleled virtual journey through the Alhambra's most iconic landmarks.

Chapter Eight
Beyond Alhambra: Exploring Granada

The Albayzin: Granada's Historic Neighbourhood

The Albayzin, Granada's historic neighborhood, captivates visitors with its rich Moorish legacy and labyrinthine alleys.tThis UNESCO World Heritage site offers a glimpse into Granada's diverse history.

Wandering through Albayzin feels like stepping back in time. The intricate layout of narrow streets, white-washed houses, and cobblestone paths reflects the area's Moorish origins. As you ascend the winding alleys, you'll encounter picturesque viewpoints providing breathtaking vistas of the Alhambra and Sierra Nevada mountains.

The heart of Albayzin is Plaza Larga, a bustling square surrounded by tapas bars and shops. It's an ideal spot to savor local delicacies while immersing yourself in the lively atmosphere. Try the local specialty, "tinto de verano," a refreshing red wine spritzer, as you absorb the authentic Andalusian charm.

Albayzin is renowned for its Moorish architecture, notably exemplified by the historic Nasrid houses. The Casa Morisca de Horno de Oro and Casa del Chapiz showcase intricate details, reflecting the Islamic influence on the region. Take a stroll through Carrera del Darro, a picturesque riverside promenade lined with charming houses, creating a timeless ambiance.

For a spiritual experience, visit the Mosque of Granada, located within Albayzin. Originally constructed as a mosque during the Nasrid dynasty, it later transformed into a church. The fusion of Islamic and Christian elements in its architecture symbolizes the region's cultural amalgamation.

As you explore, notice the vibrant street art adorning Albayzin's walls. Local artists use the neighborhood as their canvas, expressing Granada's dynamic cultural identity through colorful murals and graffiti.

Don't miss the Albayzin's evenings, when the neighborhood comes alive with the sounds of flamenco. Numerous venues offer authentic flamenco performances, providing an intimate and passionate glimpse into this traditional Andalusian art form.

A hike up to the Mirador de San Nicolás is essential. From this viewpoint, witness the Alhambra's silhouette against the backdrop of the Sierra Nevada. It's a photographer's paradise and a prime spot for appreciating the interplay of light and shadows over the iconic palace.

For a tranquil escape, explore the Generalife Gardens, an extension of the Alhambra located on the outskirts of Albayzin. These lush gardens boast fountains, flower beds, and terraces, offering a serene retreat with stunning views of Granada.

Albayzin's allure extends beyond its historic sites. The neighborhood boasts a vibrant local market, where you can immerse yourself in the daily life of Granada's residents. Sample fresh produce, regional cheeses, and aromatic spices while interacting with friendly vendors.

Exploring the Albayzin's Narrow Streets and Stunning Views

This enchanting neighborhood, perched on a hill across from the Alhambra, offers not only a step back in time but also breathtaking views that will leave you spellbound.

The labyrinthine layout of Albayzin's streets, reminiscent of its Moorish past, invites exploration. Cobblestone paths wind their way through whitewashed houses adorned with vibrant bougainvillea, creating a picturesque scene at every turn. As you navigate the intricate alleys, each step feels like a discovery, revealing hidden corners and charming details that define the neighborhood's character.

One of the highlights of Albayzin is the Mirador de San Nicolás, a viewpoint that has become synonymous with postcard-perfect views of the Alhambra.

As you ascend towards this iconic spot, the narrow streets open up to panoramic vistas, offering an unparalleled perspective of the majestic palace against the backdrop of the Sierra Nevada mountains. It's a view that captures the essence of Granada's allure – a seamless blend of history, architecture, and natural beauty.

The Mirador de San Nicolás isn't just a scenic viewpoint; it's a gathering place where locals and visitors come together to soak in the mesmerizing sunset over the Alhambra. As the golden hour bathes the palace in warm hues, the atmosphere becomes magical.

Musicians strum guitars, capturing the spirit of Flamenco, and artists set up easels to immortalize the scene on canvas. The energy is palpable, creating a sense of camaraderie among those fortunate enough to witness this daily spectacle.

Descending from the Mirador, the narrow streets beckon you to explore further. The Carrera del Darro, a riverside promenade, offers a delightful stroll along the Darro River.

Admire the historic houses, some dating back to the Nasrid era, as they seemingly cling to the hillside. The sound of flowing water accompanies your walk, creating a serene ambiance that contrasts with the lively energy of the nearby Plaza Nueva.

Albayzin's narrow streets are not just a means of getting from one point to another; they are an invitation to get lost in the charm of the past. Discover hidden squares like Plaza Larga, where locals gather to socialize, and traditional tapas bars serve up authentic Andalusian flavors.

Embrace the spontaneity of Albayzin's streets, where each corner reveals a new perspective, a different angle of the Alhambra, or a glimpse into daily life in this historic neighbourhood.

Venture into Albayzin, and you'll encounter architectural gems that embody its rich history. The Casa Morisca de Horno de Oro and Casa del Chapiz showcase the Moorish influence with their intricate designs and geometric patterns. These historic houses offer a glimpse into the lifestyle of Granada's past residents, enriching your understanding of the city's cultural tapestry.

As you meander through Albayzin, take note of the vibrant street art adorning the walls. Local artists use the neighborhood as their canvas, adding a contemporary layer to the historical surroundings. Murals and graffiti tell stories of identity, resistance, and celebration, providing a modern perspective on the neighborhood's dynamic spirit.

The Sacromonte: Flamenco and Gypsy Culture

As you venture beyond the Alhambra into this unique enclave, you are welcomed into a world where the spirit of Andalusia comes alive through passionate performances, cave dwellings, and a rich Gypsy heritage.

Sacromonte's most renowned feature is undoubtedly its cave houses, carved into the hillsides. These distinctive dwellings provide not only a fascinating glimpse into a traditional way of life but also a unique setting for experiencing authentic Flamenco performances.

Walking through the narrow, winding streets, the cave entrances beckon, inviting you to explore the heart of Sacromonte's cultural identity.

Flamenco, the soulful and expressive art form, finds its home in Sacromonte. The neighborhood resonates with the haunting melodies of guitar strings, rhythmic footwork, and impassioned vocals.

The intimate cave venues, dimly lit and exuding a sense of history, host Flamenco shows that transport you to the very essence of Andalusian culture. The emotive performances, often spontaneous and filled with raw energy, capture the deep emotions embedded in Flamenco, making it an immersive experience for visitors.

For an authentic Flamenco encounter, venture to venues like Venta El Gallo or Zambra Maria La Canastera, where the intimate setting and passionate performances create an unforgettable atmosphere.

The artists, deeply rooted in Gypsy traditions, weave a narrative through their movements, creating an emotional connection that transcends language barriers. Sacromonte's caves transform into stages where Flamenco, a living expression of Gypsy culture, is not just witnessed but felt in every beat and gesture.

Beyond the music and dance, Sacromonte offers a glimpse into the enduring Gypsy heritage. The Museo Cuevas del Sacromonte provides a cultural journey through the history of the neighborhood, showcasing traditional artifacts, photographs, and insights into Gypsy life. As you navigate through the museum, you gain a deeper appreciation for the resilience and cultural richness of the Sacromonte community.

Sacromonte is not only about Flamenco and Gypsy culture; it's a place where history, nature, and artistic expression converge. The neighborhood's elevated position offers stunning panoramic views of Granada and the Alhambra, adding an extra layer of enchantment to your visit. The combination of the Alhambra's silhouette against the sunset sky and the rhythmic beats of Flamenco in the air creates a sensory symphony that defines Sacromonte's allure.

To fully immerse yourself in the Gypsy spirit, consider exploring the Sacromonte Abbey. This historic monastery, perched atop the hills, offers a serene retreat amidst the lively energy of the neighbourhood. The Abbey, with its tranquil gardens and captivating views, provides a moment of reflection and respite, allowing you to appreciate the spiritual aspect of Sacromonte beyond its cultural vibrancy.

Tapas Bars and Culinary Delights in Granada

Tapas culture in Granada is a cherished tradition that goes beyond mere sustenance – it's a way of life. Unlike many places where tapas may be offered as complimentary snacks, Granada stands out for its unique tradition of providing a free tapa with every drink. This delightful practice transforms a casual evening of drinks into a culinary adventure, where each round unveils a new and delectable surprise.

Venture into the Albayzin, Sacromonte, or the city center, and you'll discover an array of tapas bars offering a diverse selection of small bites that range from traditional to innovative.

One of the gems nestled in the narrow streets of the Albayzin is Bodegas Castañeda. Established in 1936, this historic tapas bar exudes charm with its wooden interiors, wine barrels, and a lively atmosphere.

Sip on a glass of local wine or vermouth, and let the complimentary tapas, which could range from olives and cheese to more elaborate dishes, tantalize your taste buds.

The vibrant Plaza Nueva in the city center is home to a variety of tapas bars, each with its own unique flair. A visit to Los Diamantes, a local favorite, reveals the essence of Granada's tapas culture.

Known for its seafood offerings, this bustling establishment serves drinks accompanied by a selection of fresh, flavorful tapas. From fried fish to marinated octopus, the offerings at Los Diamantes showcase the diverse culinary expertise that Granada has to offer.

A short stroll to Calle Navas, often referred to as "Tapas Street," leads you to a lively strip where one tapas bar seamlessly blends into the next. At Taberna El Sur, the atmosphere is convivial, and the tapas are nothing short of culinary delights.

Enjoy a glass of local Alhambra beer or a refreshing tinto de verano, and relish in the parade of inventive tapas that accompany your drink. The artful presentation and diverse flavors elevate the experience, making it a testament to Granada's culinary prowess.

If you are seeking a fusion of traditional and modern tapas, the Mercado de San Agustín is a must-visit. This vibrant market, nestled in the heart of the city, is a treasure trove of fresh produce, local specialties, and a tapestry of flavors.

Inside the market, you'll find bars like Bar de San Agustín, where the chefs seamlessly blend modern techniques with traditional ingredients to create tapas that are as visually appealing as they are delicious. From Iberian ham croquettes to grilled octopus with romesco sauce, the offerings reflect the culinary innovation thriving in Granada.

A journey to Sacromonte introduces you to tapas bars with a distinct Gypsy flair. In Bodegas Castilla, the intimate setting and the fusion of Flamenco and tapas create a unique sensory experience.

Savor the earthy flavors of regional cheeses, cured meats, and olives, all while immersing yourself in the rhythmic beats of Flamenco. The harmonious blend of food and music captures the soul of Granada's cultural richness.

In Granada, tapas extend beyond the confines of bars and spill onto the streets during lively tapas routes and festivals. The Tapeo de Cervantes, an annual event celebrating the art of tapas, transforms the city into a gastronomic playground.

Join the locals as they navigate from one establishment to another, savoring an array of inventive tapas paired with local wines and beers. The Tapeo de Cervantes encapsulates the communal spirit and culinary creativity that define Granada's tapas scene.

Beyond the traditional offerings, Granada boasts avant-garde tapas bars that push culinary boundaries. Pioneros, located in the Realejo neighbourhood, is at the forefront of this gastronomic movement.

Here, you'll encounter tapas that are more akin to edible art – intricately crafted, visually stunning, and bursting with innovative flavours. The tasting menus, complemented by carefully selected wines, showcase the culinary evolution that Granada embraces while staying rooted in its rich gastronomic heritage.

Chapter Nine
Day Trips from Granada: Unveiling Nearby Gems

The Sierra Nevada: Spain's Pristine Mountain Range

Rising majestically on the southern horizon of Spain, the Sierra Nevada stands as a pristine and awe-inspiring mountain range, offering a captivating retreat for those seeking both natural beauty and outdoor adventures. Beyond the historic walls of the Alhambra, the Sierra Nevada unfolds as a picturesque haven, where rugged peaks, lush valleys, and snow-capped summits beckon travelers into a world of unparalleled scenic splendor.

Stretching across the provinces of Granada and Almería, the Sierra Nevada is not just a mountain range; it's a sanctuary for nature enthusiasts, hikers, and winter sports aficionados.

The crown jewel of the range is Mulhacén, the highest peak in mainland Spain, soaring to an elevation of 3,479 meters (11,414 feet). As you ascend its slopes, the air becomes crisper, and panoramic views of the surrounding landscapes unfold, revealing a tapestry of forests, meadows, and dramatic rock formations.

Exploring the Sierra Nevada in summer unveils a landscape adorned with wildflowers, alpine lakes, and hiking trails that wind through diverse ecosystems.

One such trail, the Vereda de la Estrella, takes you through pine forests and past pristine lakes to reach the summit of Mulhacén. The journey is a testament to the range's biodiversity, as ibexes graze on mountain slopes, and eagles soar overhead, creating a symphony of natural wonders.

If you are seeking a more leisurely experience, the Alpujarra region at the southern foothills of the Sierra Nevada offers charming villages nestled against the mountainside.

Pampaneira, Bubión, and Capileira showcase traditional Alpujarran architecture, with flat-roofed houses and winding cobblestone streets. As you wander through these villages, you'll encounter terraced farmlands, ancient irrigation channels, and a profound sense of tranquility that defines life in the shadow of the Sierra Nevada.

The Sierra Nevada's allure extends into the winter months when the mountains don a white cloak of snow, transforming the region into a haven for winter sports enthusiasts.

The ski resort of Sierra Nevada, just a short drive from Granada, offers a playground for skiers and snowboarders. Boasting over 100 kilometers of slopes and modern facilities, the resort caters to both beginners and seasoned winter sports enthusiasts. The thrill of gliding down the pristine slopes, surrounded by the stunning mountain scenery, is an experience that leaves an indelible mark on visitors.

Apart from its recreational offerings, the Sierra Nevada holds a unique ecological significance. The range is home to the endemic Spanish ibex, a symbol of the region's wildlife. As you traverse the mountain trails, you might catch sight of these agile creatures gracefully navigating the rocky terrain.

The diverse flora and fauna, including rare species adapted to the high-altitude conditions, contribute to the Sierra Nevada's designation as a UNESCO Biosphere Reserve.

For avid birdwatchers, the Sierra Nevada provides a haven to observe a variety of avian species. The Spanish Imperial Eagle, one of the rarest raptors in Europe, finds refuge in the mountains.

The skies above the Sierra Nevada come alive with the soaring wings of eagles, vultures, and falcons, creating a mesmerizing spectacle for those attuned to the rhythms of nature.

The Sierra Nevada isn't only a destination for the active traveler; it's also a place for quiet contemplation and spiritual connection. The ascent to the Veleta Peak, the second-highest peak in the range, offers an opportunity for reflection as you stand amid the silent grandeur of the mountains.

The panoramic views from this vantage point stretch across the vast landscapes, revealing the beauty that inspired poets, artists, and nature lovers throughout the ages.

As the sun sets behind the Sierra Nevada, casting a warm glow over the snow-capped peaks, a sense of serenity envelops the mountains. The interplay of light and shadows creates a canvas of ever-changing colors, from vibrant oranges to deep purples, making each sunset a unique and contemplative experience.

Whether witnessed from the mountain summits or the quaint villages of the Alpujarra, the Sierra Nevada's sunsets are a poetic culmination of a day spent in the embrace of nature.

The Alpujarras: Picturesque Villages and Natural Beauty

Situated on the southern slopes of the Sierra Nevada, the Alpujarras unfolds as a breathtaking tapestry of picturesque villages and natural wonders, offering a serene escape just beyond the historic allure of the Alhambra.

This captivating region, steeped in Moorish history and framed by rugged mountain landscapes, beckons travelers into a world where time seems to stand still, and the beauty of the countryside is harmoniously woven into the fabric of everyday life.

The Alpujarras, divided into the High Alpujarra and the Low Alpujarra, is a region of captivating contrasts. The High Alpujarra, with its steep mountainous terrain, is home to timeless villages perched on the hillsides, each with a unique charm.

Among these, Pampaneira, Bubión, and Capileira stand out as jewels of traditional Alpujarran architecture. Whitewashed houses with flat roofs, narrow winding streets, and vibrant geranium-filled balconies create a postcard-perfect scene against the backdrop of the Sierra Nevada.

Pampaneira, the first of the trio, welcomes visitors with its lively artisan shops, where locally crafted goods, from intricate textiles to handmade ceramics, showcase the skilled craftsmanship that defines the region.

Wandering through the narrow streets, the aroma of chestnut and almond treats wafts from local bakeries, enticing you to savor the sweet flavors of the Alpujarras.

Bubión, the second village, unfolds with a more tranquil ambiance. Stroll through its quiet streets, and you'll encounter traditional Alpujarran houses adorned with colorful flowers.

The village square, surrounded by charming cafes and small shops, invites you to savor the unhurried pace of life in the mountains. Bubión's allure lies in its simplicity, where the beauty of the natural surroundings merges seamlessly with the architecture and daily rhythms of its residents.

Capileira, the highest of the trio, stands as a gateway to the majestic landscapes of the Sierra Nevada. From its elevated position, the village offers panoramic views of the Poqueira Gorge and the snow-capped peaks beyond.

A starting point for hikes and explorations into the mountains, Capileira is a haven for nature enthusiasts seeking both tranquility and adventure.

The charm of the Low Alpujarra, characterized by terraced farmlands and verdant valleys, provides a stark yet harmonious contrast to the ruggedness of the High Alpujarra. Villages like Órgiva and Lanjarón offer a different perspective on Alpujarran life.

Órgiva, nestled in the fertile Guadalfeo Valley, boasts a vibrant market where locals and visitors alike converge to explore stalls laden with fresh produce, artisanal crafts, and regional delights. The town's diverse community, with a blend of locals and expatriates, contributes to its dynamic atmosphere.

Lanjarón, renowned for its natural springs and spa culture, adds a touch of relaxation to the Alpujarras experience. The Balneario de Lanjarón, a historic spa dating back to the 18th century, invites you to indulge in the therapeutic properties of the local mineral-rich waters.

Surrounded by lush gardens and set against the backdrop of the Sierra Nevada, the spa provides a tranquil retreat where the healing powers of nature seamlessly blend with traditional spa rituals.

Beyond the charming villages, the Alpujarras are a haven for hikers and nature lovers. The GR-7 long-distance trail winds through the region, offering opportunities for exploration and immersion in the natural beauty that defines the area.

Hike through ancient chestnut forests, traverse terraced landscapes, and encounter hidden waterfalls as you follow the trails that crisscross the mountains. The diversity of flora, from aromatic herbs to wild orchids, adds to the sensory richness of the experience.

One of the highlights of the Alpujarras is the Poqueira Gorge, a dramatic canyon carved by the Poqueira River. The hike from Capileira to the villages of Pampaneira and Bubión, following the course of the river, provides a glimpse into the rugged grandeur of the landscape. Traverse ancient footpaths and marvel at the terraced fields clinging to the mountainsides, showcasing the ingenuity of traditional Alpujarran agriculture.

As the sun sets behind the Sierra Nevada, casting a warm glow over the villages and valleys, the Alpujarras reveal a different kind of magic. The tranquil evenings, with the scent of mountain herbs in the air, invite you to savor the simplicity of life in this timeless region.

The night sky, unpolluted by urban lights, unfolds a celestial canvas, offering a breathtaking display of stars that adds to the enchantment of the Alpujarras.

The Caves of Guadix: Underground Wonders

Beneath the sun-drenched landscape of Guadix in the province of Granada lies a hidden marvel that defies conventional notions of habitation – the Caves of Guadix. Carved into the soft sedimentary rock, these subterranean dwellings offer an enchanting journey into a unique way of life, where centuries-old traditions seamlessly blend with modern comforts.

Beyond the timeless allure of the Alhambra, the Caves of Guadix emerge as underground wonders, inviting visitors to explore a world shaped by both nature and human ingenuity.

Guadix, with its distinctive white houses nestled against the backdrop of the Sierra Nevada, sets the stage for this subterranean adventure. The caves, known locally as "cuevas," are scattered across the hillsides surrounding the town, forming a surreal landscape that seems almost otherworldly.

As you venture into this labyrinth of earthen dwellings, you're transported into a realm where the temperature remains moderate year-round, offering respite from the scorching Andalusian summers and chilly winters.

The history of the Caves of Guadix dates back to ancient times when Berber settlers first dug into the soft tuff rock to create shelter from the elements. Over the centuries, this practice evolved, and the caves became homes, each uniquely reflecting the creativity and adaptability of their inhabitants.

Today, these caves blend seamlessly with the natural contours of the landscape, creating a harmonious integration of human dwellings and the earth itself.

Exploring the caves unveils a variety of architectural styles, from simple troglodyte shelters to more elaborate, multi-roomed cave houses. The interiors often feature whitewashed walls, providing a sense of brightness and spaciousness.

Some caves are adorned with traditional Andalusian tiles and rustic furnishings, preserving a link to the region's cultural heritage. The ingenious design of these underground dwellings maintains a constant temperature, ensuring coolness in summer and warmth in winter.

One of the remarkable aspects of the Caves of Guadix is the vibrant community that thrives within this subterranean world. Families have passed down these caves through generations, and many are still inhabited today.

The cave dwellers, known as "troglodytes," have embraced modern amenities while preserving the traditions of their ancestors. As you wander through the cave neighborhoods, you might catch glimpses of troglodyte life – laundry drying in the sun, pots of vibrant flowers decorating entrances, and locals engaged in lively conversations on their doorsteps.

For a deeper understanding of troglodyte life, a visit to the Cuevas de Guadix Museum provides insight into the history, architecture, and daily routines of cave dwellers.

The museum, housed in a series of interconnected caves, showcases artifacts, photographs, and displays that bring to life the rich heritage of this unique community.

It's an immersive experience that complements the exploration of the actual caves, offering a comprehensive perspective on the symbiotic relationship between the troglodytes and their subterranean abodes.

Several cave houses in Guadix have been converted into charming accommodations, allowing visitors to experience the allure of troglodyte living firsthand. These cave hotels, such as Cuevas Pedro Antonio de Alarcon and Cuevas La Granja, offer a unique blend of modern comforts within ancient rock walls.

Staying in a cave hotel becomes an enchanting experience, where the natural quietude and coolness of the caves create an atmosphere of tranquility and relaxation.

Guadix celebrates its subterranean heritage annually with the Fiesta de las Cuadras, a festival that brings the troglodyte community together. The event features cave tours, cultural performances, and a vibrant market showcasing local crafts and gastronomy.

Visitors during the festival gain a deeper appreciation for the caves' role in shaping the identity of Guadix and fostering a sense of community among its residents.

Beyond the residential caves, Guadix boasts impressive cave churches and hermitages that add a spiritual dimension to this subterranean landscape. The Ermita Nueva de la Virgen de la Piedad, a cave hermitage built into the rock, stands as a testament to the troglodyte community's religious traditions. The simplicity and natural beauty of these cave sanctuaries provide a unique backdrop for contemplation and reflection.

Chapter Ten
Conclusion

Making the Most of Your Alhambra Experience

To truly make the most of your Alhambra experience, it's essential to approach this architectural marvel with a blend of anticipation, exploration, and appreciation for the rich history and intricate details that unfold within its walls.

From strategic planning to immersing yourself in the nuances of Nasrid artistry, here's to ensure your visit to the Alhambra becomes an unforgettable journey.

Strategic Planning:

Begin your Alhambra adventure by strategically planning your visit. Tickets are often limited, and demand is high, so it's advisable to book well in advance.

Choose a time slot that aligns with your preferences – whether it's the ethereal glow of morning light, the warm hues of sunset, or the mystical ambiance of the evening. Plan to arrive early to explore the Nasrid Palaces when they are less crowded, allowing for a more intimate experience.

Nasrid Palaces:

The crown jewel of the Alhambra, the Nasrid Palaces, demands dedicated exploration. Marvel at the intricate stucco work, the delicately carved wooden ceilings, and the serene courtyards that embody the essence of Islamic architecture.

Take your time in the Court of the Lions, where the central fountain becomes the focal point of this symmetrical masterpiece. Allow the sheer beauty of the Palacios Nazaríes to transport you back in time, imagining the opulence and refinement that once filled these halls.

Generalife Gardens:

Transition from the regal interiors to the refreshing embrace of the Generalife Gardens. These meticulously landscaped gardens offer a sensory escape, with fragrant flowers, serene water features, and strategically placed architectural elements.

Stroll through the lush pathways, appreciating the interplay of light and shadow, and savor the panoramic views of the Alhambra from the Generalife Palace. The tranquility of these gardens provides a serene counterpoint to the grandeur of the Nasrid Palaces.

Alcazaba Fortress:

Ascend to the Alcazaba Fortress, the oldest part of the Alhambra complex. From its watchtowers, absorb breathtaking views of Granada and the surrounding mountains.

Explore the military quarters, where history unfolds in the form of well-preserved battlements, towers, and gates. The Alcazaba offers not only historical insights but also an opportunity to appreciate the strategic importance of this fortress in the medieval era.

Palacio de Carlos V:

Visit the Palacio de Carlos V, a Renaissance masterpiece within the Alhambra complex. Although its style starkly contrasts with the Nasrid architecture, the palace provides a fascinating glimpse into the evolving history of the Alhambra.

The circular courtyard and the museum housed within the palace showcase artifacts and exhibits that enrich your understanding of the site's multifaceted history.

The Nasrid Artisan Quarter:

Venture beyond the major attractions to discover the Nasrid Artisan Quarter. Tucked away in the Albayzin neighborhood, this area is home to workshops where skilled artisans practice traditional crafts.

From intricate tilework to woodcarving and metalwork, witnessing these artisans at work adds a layer of appreciation for the craftsmanship that defined the Nasrid era. Consider acquiring a handmade souvenir as a tangible memento of your Alhambra experience.

Time for Contemplation:

Allocate moments for quiet contemplation within the Alhambra's precincts. Find a secluded spot, perhaps in the tranquil corners of the Generalife or amidst the geometric patterns of the Nasrid Palaces.

Absorb the ambience, listen to the soothing sound of water, and reflect on the profound cultural and historical significance encapsulated within these walls. The Alhambra has a unique ability to evoke a sense of wonder and contemplation.

Sunset at Mirador de San Nicolás:

Conclude your Alhambra day with a visit to the Mirador de San Nicolás. This iconic viewpoint, situated in the Albayzin neighborhood, provides a spectacular panorama of the Alhambra against the Sierra Nevada.

As the sun sets, casting a warm glow on the palace, you'll witness a transformative scene that encapsulates the enchantment of Granada. It's a moment that serves as a poetic farewell to the Alhambra, leaving an indelible mark on your memory.

Insider Tips for an Enriching Visit

Early Morning Advantage:

Arriving early provides a distinct advantage, especially when exploring the Nasrid Palaces. Early morning sunlight bathes the intricate details in a soft glow, creating an ethereal atmosphere that amplifies the beauty of the stucco work and tile patterns. With fewer crowds, you can relish the serenity of the Nasrid Palaces, allowing for a more immersive and contemplative experience.

Evening Visit to the Nasrid Palaces:

Consider booking a late afternoon or evening time slot for the Nasrid Palaces. As the day winds down, the ambient light transforms the palaces into a mesmerizing display of shadows and highlights.

The tranquil atmosphere during these hours lends an almost mystical quality to the Nasrid Palaces, providing a unique perspective that differs from daytime visits.

Generalife Gardens in the Morning:

For a refreshing start to your day, explore the Generalife Gardens in the morning. The gardens, resplendent with vibrant flowers and serene water features, offer a sensory escape. With fewer visitors early in the day, you can relish the tranquil ambiance and appreciate the delicate interplay of light and shadow that defines the Generalife experience.

The Alhambra Night Visit:

Take advantage of the special nighttime visits to the Nasrid Palaces, which provide an enchanting ambiance under the moonlight.

The reduced visitor numbers and carefully orchestrated lighting create an intimate setting, allowing you to appreciate the Nasrid Palaces in a different, more mystical light. Night visits are an exclusive opportunity to witness the Alhambra in a quieter, more magical setting.

Guided Tours for In-Depth Insights:

Engage in a guided tour to gain deeper insights into the Alhambra's history and symbolism. Knowledgeable guides can unveil the stories behind the intricate decorations, share anecdotes about the Nasrid rulers, and provide a comprehensive understanding of the architectural evolution of the site. A well-informed guide can transform your visit into a rich educational experience.

Audio Guides for a Self-Paced Tour:

If you prefer a more self-paced exploration, consider utilizing audio guides available at the site. These guides provide detailed commentary at key points, offering a wealth of information without the constraints of a group tour. This allows you to absorb the details at your own pace and spend more time at areas that resonate with you.

Explore Beyond the Main Attractions:

While the Nasrid Palaces and Generalife are must-visit highlights, take the time to explore lesser-known areas within the Alhambra complex. The Alcazaba Fortress, the Palace of

Carlos V, and the Nasrid Artisan Quarter offer distinctive insights into the multifaceted history of the site. Venture into these lesser-explored corners to discover hidden gems that contribute to the richness of your visit.

Nasrid Artisan Quarter Workshops:

Delve into the Nasrid Artisan Quarter, located in the Albayzin neighborhood adjacent to the Alhambra. Here, workshops showcase traditional crafts such as tile making, wood carving, and metalwork. Visiting these workshops provides a fascinating glimpse into the continuation of ancient artistic traditions and allows you to witness skilled artisans at work.

Enjoy a Moment of Contemplation:

Amidst the grandeur and intricacies of the Alhambra, allocate moments for quiet contemplation. Find a secluded spot, perhaps in one of the courtyards or gardens, and soak in the ambiance.

Reflect on the historical significance, cultural richness, and the sheer beauty that envelops you. These moments of stillness amidst the vibrant tapestry of the Alhambra enhance the overall experience.

Mirador de San Nicolás for Spectacular Views:

Extend your Alhambra experience by visiting the Mirador de San Nicolás in the Albayzin neighborhood. This iconic viewpoint provides unparalleled panoramic views of the Alhambra against the Sierra Nevada.

Sunset is a particularly magical time to witness the Alhambra bathed in warm hues, creating a scene that encapsulates the enchantment of Granada.

Preserving Alhambra's Legacy for Future Generations

Preserving the legacy of the Alhambra, a gem that transcends time and bears witness to centuries of artistry, cultural exchange, and historical significance, is a noble undertaking crucial for future generations.

This architectural masterpiece,has stood as a testament to the enduring legacy of Islamic architecture and Moorish culture. Ensuring its conservation involves a delicate balance of meticulous restoration, technological innovation, and a commitment to safeguarding the site's unique historical and artistic value.

Restoration as a Form of Artistic Reverence:

Preserving the Alhambra for future generations begins with a deep understanding of its artistic nuances and historical context. The ongoing restoration efforts within the Nasrid Palaces, Generalife Gardens, and other sections of the complex aim not only to address structural concerns but also to revive the intricate details that define its beauty.

Teams of skilled craftsmen, conservators, and historians collaborate to meticulously restore delicate stucco work, colorful tile mosaics, and ornate wooden carvings to their original splendor.

This restoration is not merely a technical process; it is an artistic endeavor rooted in reverence for the craftsmanship of the Nasrid artisans. By employing traditional techniques and materials, restorers pay homage to the original spirit of the Alhambra.

Each meticulous repair is a brushstroke that contributes to the ongoing narrative of preserving the site's legacy, ensuring that the Alhambra remains an authentic reflection of its historical grandeur.

Harnessing Technology to Safeguard Heritage:

In the quest to preserve the Alhambra's legacy, technology emerges as a powerful ally. Cutting-edge advancements in digital documentation, 3D scanning, and virtual reality are employed to create comprehensive records of the site. These digital archives not only serve as invaluable references for ongoing restoration but also provide an immersive experience for virtual visitors worldwide.

High-resolution scans capture the intricate details of the Nasrid Palaces, allowing experts to study the subtle nuances of design and construction. Virtual tours enable people from every corner of the globe to explore the Alhambra's beauty in unprecedented detail.

Embracing technology ensures that the legacy of the Alhambra transcends physical boundaries, making its cultural and historical wealth accessible to a global audience.

Sustainable Practices for Environmental Harmony:

Preserving the Alhambra's legacy involves a commitment to sustainable practices that ensure the site's longevity while harmonizing with its natural surroundings. Conservation efforts extend beyond architectural elements to include the delicate ecosystems within the Generalife Gardens.

The careful management of water resources, sustainable gardening practices, and a commitment to biodiversity contribute to the environmental harmony of the site.

Incorporating eco-friendly measures not only safeguards the natural beauty of the Alhambra but also aligns with the ethos of sustainability for future generations.

The commitment to environmental responsibility is a testament to the holistic approach to heritage preservation, recognizing that the Alhambra's legacy extends beyond its architectural splendor to encompass the broader ecological context.

Educational Initiatives for Cultural Continuity:

Preserving the legacy of the Alhambra necessitates a proactive engagement with educational initiatives that foster cultural continuity. Programs designed to educate schoolchildren, scholars, and the general public about the historical, architectural, and cultural significance of the Alhambra play a pivotal role.

Guided tours, educational workshops, and outreach efforts contribute to cultivating a sense of appreciation and responsibility for this cultural treasure.

By instilling a deep understanding of the Alhambra's legacy in younger generations, these educational initiatives ensure that future custodians will inherit not only the physical site but also the knowledge and passion necessary for its preservation.

The Alhambra becomes a living classroom where the lessons of history, art, and cultural diversity are passed down through the ages.

Responsible Tourism and Visitor Engagement:

Preserving the Alhambra's legacy involves striking a balance between welcoming visitors and safeguarding the site from the impact of mass tourism.

Implementing responsible tourism practices, including controlled visitor numbers, timed entries, and educational guidelines, ensures that the Alhambra remains a sustainable and respectful destination.

Visitor engagement initiatives, such as curated exhibitions, interactive displays, and informative signage, enhance the visitor experience while fostering a sense of responsibility.

Encouraging mindfulness among visitors about the significance of the Alhambra and the role they play in its preservation creates a collective commitment to protecting this cultural jewel for generations to come.

Collaboration and International Cooperation:

Preserving the Alhambra's legacy transcends borders and requires collaborative efforts on an international scale. Partnerships with heritage preservation organizations, academic institutions, and experts from various fields contribute to a holistic approach to conservation.

Sharing knowledge, best practices, and technological innovations ensures that the Alhambra benefits from a diverse range of expertise.

International cooperation also opens avenues for collaborative research, facilitating a deeper understanding of the Alhambra's historical and cultural significance. The exchange of ideas and collaborative projects contribute to a global network dedicated to safeguarding cultural heritage for the enrichment of future generations.

Printed in Great Britain
by Amazon